Foster
n Hird
Jones
Mahon
Peter Maggs
Carmen Santos Maldonado
Priscilla Osborne
Jeremy Page
Jenny Roden
David Seymour
Katherine Stannett

Inside Out

Resource
Pack

Pre-intermediate

MACMILLAN

Macmillan Education
Between Towns Road, Oxford OX4 3PP
A division of Macmillan Publishers Limited
Companies and representatives throughout the world

ISBN 0 333 97589 8

Text © Sue Kay, Vaughan Jones and Philip Kerr 2002
Design and illustration © Macmillan Publishers Limited 2002

First published 2002

Permission to copy

The material in this book is copyright. However, the publisher grants permission for copies to be made without fee on those pages marked with the PHOTOCOPIABLE symbol.

Private purchasers may make copies for their own use or for use by classes of which they are in charge; school purchasers may make copies for use, within and by the staff and students of the school only. This permission does not extend to additional schools or branches of an institution, who should purchase a separate master copy of the book for their own use.

For copying in any other circumstances, prior permission in writing must be obtained from Macmillan Publishers Limited.

Designed by Sarah Nicholson
Illustrations by Kathy Baxendale pp2B, pp14A, pp16B;
Mark Draisey pp3A, pp17B; Mark Duffin pp18A; Mark Ruffle pp13B, pp16C; Bill Piggins pp5A, pp9A, pp17A; Peter Maggs pp1B
Cover design by Andrew Oliver

Printed and bound in Great Britain by Martins the Printers

Introduction

This Resource Pack for teachers contains thirty-seven practice activities for pre-intermediate students of English. It is designed to be used with *Inside Out* Pre-intermediate Student's Book.

Ten practising teachers have contributed activities, so you'll find a wealth of different ideas for practising skills and specific language points. All the activities have been tested in the classroom.

Using the worksheets

You can use the activities in many different ways. For example:
- to extend the lessons in the Student's Book
- as revision of points in the Student's Book, for example at the beginning of the following lesson
- to supplement other courses
- as a basis for standby lessons

How to use the Resource Pack

Each activity consists of one photocopiable worksheet original. The originals have been designed for maximum clarity when photocopied. However, if your photocopier has the facility to enlarge, you may sometimes find this useful – particularly for board games or worksheets which are to be cut up into cards.

Each original appears on the right-hand page, with teacher's notes on the left-hand page so that you can see them both at the same time. The notes explain the aims of the activity, describe the task, tell you what you need to do to prepare and then give a step-by-step lesson plan, This makes them easy to use if you haven't been teaching long, but it is also a terrific time-saver for experienced teachers. Regard the lesson plans as a starting point. As you use the worksheets you'll find your own ways of making the best of them in class. Some of the worksheets need cutting up into sections. To make these easier to handle in the classroom, glue them onto small pieces of card – index cards or blank business cards, available from most stationers, are ideal. After the lesson, file the cards in an envelope for the next time you use them. Write the name of the activity and the number of cards on the outside.

Some activities require multiple sets of cards. In these cases, it is a good idea to distinguish each set in some way. Put a different mark, preferably in different coloured pens, on the cards from each set. Or, even better, photocopy them on different coloured papers. This will save you time when you re-file them at the end of the lesson.

Over to you

If you have any comments about *Inside Out*, you will find a feedback form on our website at *www.insideout.net*, where you can also register to receive extra teaching materials free every week by e-mail. Your opinions will help to shape our future publishing.

Contents

Worksheet	Timing	Task	Aim (lexis, grammar, pronunciation, skills)
1A *What's in a name?*	20–25 minutes	To find out information about people.	To practise question forms and word order in questions.
1B *Family party*	15–20 minutes	To memorise details in a picture and answer questions about it.	To practise question word order and *look / look like*.
2A *Categorise*	20 minutes	To put words into the correct category and divide them into countables and uncountables.	To revise and reinforce vocabulary, especially countable and uncountable nouns, from unit 2 of *Inside Out* Pre-intermediate Student's Book
2B *Worldsearch*	30–40 minutes	To write clues for a crossword and to complete it.	To practise country names and their stress patterns.
3A *Friday the 13th*	20 minutes	To write about a picture	To practise past continuous.
3B *Childhood sweethearts*	30–40 minutes	To read a jigsaw text and to communicate to find the differences.	To practise the past tenses.
4A *Broken sentences*	15 minutes	To match parts of broken sentences so that they make one complete sentence.	To review the use of comparatives and vocabulary for describing fitness.
4B *Numbers, numbers, numbers*	30 minutes	To ask and answer general knowledge/trivia questions.	To consolidate and practise numbers and superlatives.
5 *A few quick questions*	30 minutes	To complete statements about classmates by mingling and asking questions.	To consolidate asking questions and the topics and language from units 1 to 4 of *Inside Out* Pre–intermediate Student's Book.
6A *Let's talk!*	30–45 minutes	To play a board game where students form questions using gerunds and infinitives.	To practise using gerunds and infinitives after particular verbs.
6B *Perfect match*	25–30 minutes	To complete information about two friends or relatives and to try to find partners for them.	To practise verbs that are followed by the gerund.
7A *Susie's party*	Up to 1 hour	To find out, by exchanging information, personal details about a person met at a party. To recall those details.	To reinforce use of the present perfect and past simple. To practise talking about jobs.
7B *Half a conversation*	30 minutes	To complete, practise and perform conversations.	To practise present perfect for time up to now and past simple for finished time.
7C *Changes*	45–60 minutes	To categorise a range of subjects according to whether they have changed completely, a little, or not at all over the past ten years.	To practise present perfect for general experience at an unspecified time in the past.
8A *Thirty-second futures*	30–40 minutes	To play a board game requiring students to talk about their futures.	To practise present continuous and *going to* for future arrangements and plans.
8B *The root of all evil*	Up to 1 hour	To read and rehearse the play in small groups. To perform the play in groups of four to the other students.	To practise pronunciation, especially stress and intonation. To reinforce *going to* and the use of the present continuous for the future
9A *Obeying the rules*	50 minutes	To identify and discuss genuine rules. To produce rules for the class.	To practise modals of obligation.
9B *Character crossword*	30 minutes	To complete a crossword by identifying opposite character adjectives.	To consolidate and practise using character adjectives.

Worksheet		Timing	Task	Aim (lexis, grammar, pronunciation, skills)
10	What's my job?	20–25 minutes	To seek information about one's 'job' and to deduce what it is.	To practise adverbs of frequency and job-related questions.
11A	Smile!	15 minutes	To play a review game in two teams.	To review lexis from the Student's Book unit by choosing the correct alternative in a sentence.
11B	Phrasal verb jokes	40 minutes	To match questions and answers of jokes.	To revise, practise and expand phrasal verbs.
12A	Manifesto	1 hour	To write a manifesto for a pressure group and to present it to the class.	To practise vocabulary connected with topical issues and to practise the language of expressing opinions.
12B	Dynamic replies	20 minutes	To reply suitably to given conversation starters.	To practise using verbs in either dynamic or stative forms in common situations.
13A	Guess my job	15–25 minutes	To talk about the activities and achievements of people in different professions over a period of time.	To practise the present perfect continuous and simple.
13B	For and since	25 minutes	Students mingle and complete a worksheet.	To practise questions with *How long ...?* + present perfect simple/continuous, and answers with *for/since*, in the context of lifestyle habits.
14A	Hello Tom, it's Paula...	30–35 minutes	To make requests and offers over the phone.	To practise offers and requests and telephone language.
14B	Where am I?	1 hour	To complete the dialogue.	To practise informal telephone conversations, requests and giving directions.
15	Find the mistake	40 minutes	To correct the grammar mistakes in twelve questions and to use these questions for discussion.	To consolidate the main language areas covered by units 11 to 14 in *Inside Out* Pre-intermediate Student's Book.
16A	Food	25 minutes	Students play a board game consisting of topics relating to food.	To improve fluency in speaking.
16B	Healthy eating	30-45 minutes	To create a menu for a health farm's restaurant.	To practise food vocabulary.
17A	Homophones	20 minutes	To write down two words with the same sound and then play a matching game in two teams.	To identify words with the same sound but different spelling.
17B	Animal stories	40 minutes	To read short animal stories and then re-tell them from memory.	To develop techniques for improving memory. To find defining relative clauses.
18A	Puzzled?	45 minutes	To ask *yes/no* questions to solve mysteries.	Practice of past perfect and other question forms.
18B	What happened?	35-40 minutes	To complete short texts using the correct tense. To sequence a series of events.	To practise narrative tenses.
19A	Then or now?	30 minutes	To compare past and present lifestyles by discussing contentious statements.	To practise *used to* + infinitive for past habits and states.
19B	Interview with a centenarian	30-40 minutes	To carry out a role-play in the form of an interview with a centenarian.	To practise *used to* + infinitive in question and answer forms.
20	Shout it out	30-40 minutes	To guess ten given items in various lexical/general knowledge categories, played as a team game.	To consolidate some of the vocabulary and topics from *Inside Out* Pre-intermediate Student's Book.

TEACHER'S NOTES

1A *What's in a name?*

Carmen Santos Maldonado

Type of activity
Speaking. Pair work.

Aim
To practise question forms and word order in questions.

Task
To find out information about people.

Preparation
Make one copy of the worksheet for each pair of students and cut it into two as indicated.

Timing
20–25 minutes.

Procedure
1 Demonstrate the activity by writing the name of a member of your family on the board.
2 Invite questions from the students about this person, guiding the questions if necessary.
3 Tell the students they are going to do the same, in pairs, according to some written instructions on a worksheet.
4 Divide the class into equal numbers of Student As and Student Bs. Give a copy of the A worksheet to Student A and a copy of B worksheet to Student B. Tell them they are not to let their partners see their worksheet.
5 Ask the students to complete the 'NAMES' section of the worksheet. They then tear off this section and exchange it with their partner.
6 Ask the students to ask their partner at least three questions about each of their partner's names. They can use the questions on their worksheets as guidance.
7 Circulate and make sure students form questions correctly.
8 When most students have finished, ask two or three students to describe one person from their partner's list.

Notes & comments
If some pairs finish early, ask them to swap partners and start again.
If you want to make this into a shorter exercise, the introductory and concluding parts (steps 1, 2 and 8) can be missed out.

1A *What's in a name?*

A

Write the first name of ...

1 your best female friend →
2 one of your neighbours →
3 a member of your family →
4 a sports personality →

NAMES

1 _____
2 _____
3 _____
4 _____

Examples of questions:

- Who / (name)?
- How / old?
- Where / live?
- Do / any sports?
- speak / English?
- What / look like?
- When / birthday?
- What / do?

Tear off this section and give it to your partner when you have written all the names.

B

Write the first name of ...

1 one of your grandparents →
2 one of your colleagues/classmates →
3 your best male friend →
4 a TV or film personality →

NAMES

1 _____
2 _____
3 _____
4 _____

Examples of questions:

- Who / (name)?
- What / look like?
- What / favourite hobby?
- How often / visit?
- Is / married?
- Have / children?
- What / at weekends?
- Have / pets?

Tear off this section and give it to your partner when you have written all the names.

1A *What's in a name?*

TEACHER'S NOTES

1B Family party

Peter Maggs

Type of activity
Memory game. Pair work.

Aims
To practise question word order and *look/look like*.

Task
To memorise details in a picture and answer questions about it.

Preparation
Make a copy of the worksheet for each student in the class.

Timing
15–20 minutes.

Procedure
1 Tell your students you are going to show them a picture and then ask them some questions about it. Tell them that they will have a time limit of two minutes and they must remember as many details in the picture as they can.
2 Give each student a copy of the worksheet. After two minutes, ask your students to turn over their pieces of paper.
3 Divide the class into pairs or small groups and tell the students you are going to ask them some questions.
4 Read out each question from the box on the right, giving students enough time to discuss the answers together. Encourage them to make a guess if they can't remember some of the details.
5 Check students' answers (maybe write them on the board) but offer no answers of your own at this stage.
6 Ask your students to check the picture again to find out the answers.
7 Check the answers in open class. The pair with the most correct answers are the winners.

Answers
1	6	8	3	15	yes
2	a glass	9	a bottle	16	a cap
3	no	10	no	17	6
4	5	11	2	18	no
5	yes	12	old	19	a (walking) stick
6	a pipe	13	flowers	20	5
7	yes	14	5		

Follow up
For homework, ask your students to find a picture with lots going on in it (in magazines or even comics) and write ten questions for it. In class, they should then test each other's memory.

Notes & comments
The picture for this activity could also be used for:
- describing people (*Ken's got a moustache. He's wearing a tie and smoking a pipe*).
- present continuous memory game (*What is Ben doing?*)

Questions
1 How many children are there?
2 What has Julian got in his hand?
3 Does Linda look happy?
4 How many people have got earrings?
5 Can Jane play the guitar?
6 What has Ken got in his mouth?
7 Does Emma wear glasses?
8 How many pictures are there on the wall?
9 What has Sue got in her hand?
10 Does Will look smart?
11 How many people have got a moustache?
12 Is Tom young or old?
13 What has Mary got in her hand?
14 How many people have got long hair?
15 Does Tim look like Ben?
16 What has Simon got on his head?
17 How many balloons are there?
18 Can Ellen sing?
19 What has Tom got in his hand?
20 How many bottles are there on the table?

INSIDE OUT *Resource Pack*

1B *Family party*

Photocopiable

TEACHER'S NOTES

2A Categorise
Katherine Stannett

Type of activity
Vocabulary. Group or pair work.

Aim
To revise and reinforce vocabulary, especially countable and uncountable nouns from unit 2 in *Inside Out* Pre-intermediate Student's Book.

Task
To put words in the correct category and divide them into countables and uncountables.

Preparation
Make one photocopy of the worksheet for each group.

Timing
20 minutes.

Procedure
1 Divide the students into pairs or small groups. Give each group a worksheet.
2 Tell students to categorise all the words on their worksheet under the eight headings. The winner is the first group to categorize all their words successfully. Monitor the activity, helping with any vocabulary problems that arise.
3 Write the eight headings on the board and ask representatives from each group to come up to the board and write the words under the headings.
4 Tell students to read through the categorized words and mark each word with a U for uncountable and a C for countable. The winner is the first group to divide all their words successfully.

Answers

transport		**drink**	
car	C	coffee	C/U
bus	C	wine	U
taxi	C	beer	C/U
traffic	U	tea	C/U
buildings		water	U
high-rise office block	C	juice	U
castle	C	**weather**	
church	C	rain	U
house	C	snow	U
geography		sunshine	U
sea	C/U	cloud	C/U
coast	C	wind	U
mountain	C	fog	U
canal	C	**countries**	
going out		Brazil	C
nightlife	U	Turkey	C
theatre	C	Malta	C
cinema	C	Ireland	C
disco	C	Greece	C
food		Egypt	C
fruit	U		
bread	U		
vegetables	C		
cake	C/U		
meat	U		
rice	U		

INSIDE OUT *Resource Pack*

2A *Categorise*

Put the words below under these headings.

transport	buildings	geography	going out
___	___	___	___
___	___	___	___
___	___	___	___
___	___	___	___

food	drink	weather	countries
___	___	___	___
___	___	___	___
___	___	___	___
___	___	___	___
___	___	___	___

beer	cloud	Ireland	sunshine
Brazil	coast	juice	taxi
bread	coffee	Malta	tea
bus	disco	meat	theatre
cake	Egypt	mountain	traffic
canal	fog	nightlife	Turkey
car	fruit	rain	vegetables
castle	Greece	rice	water
church	high-rise office block	sea	wind
cinema	house	snow	wine

Now decide which are countable and which are uncountable.

© Sue Kay, Vaughan Jones and Philip Kerr, 2002. Published by Macmillan Publishers Limited. This sheet may be photocopied and used within the class. **Photocopiable**

TEACHER'S NOTES

2B Worldsearch
Peter Maggs

Type of activity
Writing. Group work. Speaking. Pair and group work.

Aims
To practise country names and their stress patterns.

Task
To write clues for a crossword and to complete it.

Preparation
One copy of the worksheet, cut in half as indicated, for each pair of students in the class. It would be very useful to have a map of the world/atlas to hand and even an encyclopaedia as a reference for students unfamiliar with some of these countries.

Timing
30–40 minutes.

Procedure
1 Write: *It is famous for wine, food and romance. There is a famous tower in the capital city.* on the board. Ask students to guess the country (*France*). Tell the students they are going to write some similar hints as clues for a crossword.
2 Divide the class into Team A and Team B. Explain that you are going to give each group the same crossword but that Team A will have the 'across' words already written in and Team B will have the 'down' words already written in. Their task is to write the clues for the words written on their crosswords.
3 Give a copy of crossword A to each student in Team A and a copy of crossword B to each student in Team B. Ask the students to work together with people in their group to write a clue for each country.
4 To help your students prepare the clues; monitor carefully and encourage them to think particularly about: a) geographical location, b) what the country produces, c) what it's famous for and d) what its capital city is called. All of these could make useful clues.
5 When they have finished writing their clues, students should work with a partner from the other group. They must not show each other their crossword.
6 Ask them to sit facing each other and take it in turns to ask their partner for clues to the missing names on their crossword.
7 When they have asked and answered all the questions and completed their crosswords, they can look at each other's paper to check.

Follow up
See the stress pattern exercise below as an optional follow up activity.
Ask students to remain with their partner to work out which country name goes into which column, according to how the country name is pronounced. Explain there is room for only three countries in each column. Monitor students closely at this stage to help any students who may be struggling.
Check answers in open class.

Answers

■▫	▫■	▫■▫
England	Japan	New Zealand
China	Brazil	Morocco
Turkey	Kuwait	Korea

■▫▫	▫■▫▫	▫▫■▫
Germany	Colombia	Venezuela
Libya	Slovakia	Argentina
Italy	Australia	Madagascar

Give one copy of this to each student in the class:

-- ✂

Put each country from your crossword in an appropriate column according to its stress pattern.

■▫	▫■	▫■▫
	Kuwait	
____	____	____
____	____	____

■▫▫	▫■▫▫	▫▫■▫
____	____	Venezuela
____	____	____
____	____	____

INSIDE OUT *Resource Pack*

2B *Worldsearch*

Write the clues.

4 <u>It's a South American country.
   It has a very strong oil industry.</u>

8 _____

12 _____

13 _____

14 _____

15 _____

16 _____

17 _____

18 _____

Across answers visible in grid:
4 VENEZUELA
8 MADAGASCAR
12 KOREA
13 ITALY
14 ENGLAND
15 JAPAN
16 KUWAIT
17 GERMANY
18 CHINA

✂ ···

Write the clues.

1 <u>It's a South American country.
   The capital city is Bogota.</u>

2 _____

3 _____

5 _____

6 _____

7 _____

9 _____

10 _____

11 _____

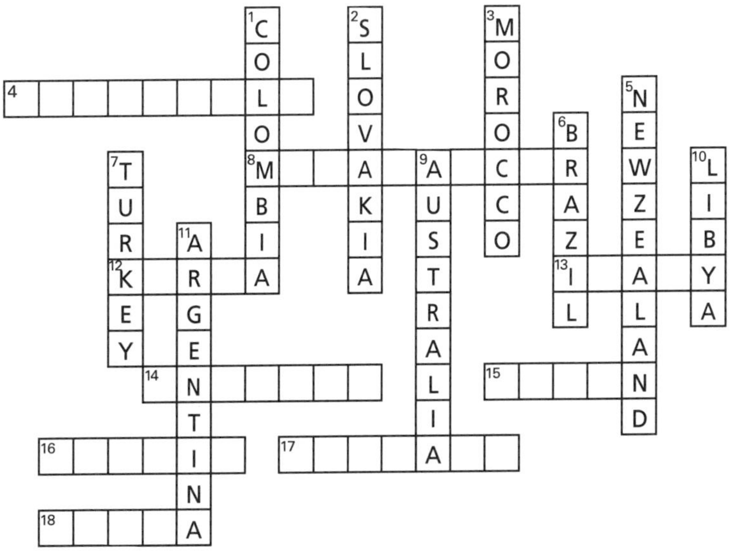

Down answers visible in grid:
1 COLOMBIA
2 SLOVAKIA
3 MOROCCO
5 NEWZEALAND
6 BRAZIL
7 TURKEY
8 MBABANE
9 AUSTRALIA
10 LIBYA
11 ARGENTINE
12 K
13 I
14 NT
15
16
17
18

© Sue Kay, Vaughan Jones and Philip Kerr, 2002. Published by Macmillan Publishers Limited. This sheet may be photocopied and used within the class.

Photocopiable

TEACHER'S NOTES

3A Friday the 13th

David Seymour

Type of activity
Writing. Pair work.

Aims
To practise past continuous.

Task
To write about a picture.

Preparation
Make one copy of the worksheet for each pair of students.

Timing
20 minutes.

Procedure
1. Write the following on the board. Elicit the missing words.
   He _____ a newspaper when the accident _____ . (was buying, happened)
2. Divide the class into pairs. Give out one copy of the picture to each pair. Ask students to work together to write sentences about the picture using the same structure.
3. Add the following sentence to the model:
   When the accident _____ , he _____ an ambulance.
   Ask students at random to read out one of their sentences. After each one ask what happened next.
4. Tell each student to choose one of the people in the picture. Elicit a few questions and answers from open pairs, e.g.:
   What were you doing when the accident happened?
   I was waiting at the bus stop.
   What did you do when the accident happened?
   I went to help.

Follow up
Friday the 13th, part 2: Students work together in groups to write about the rest of the day for the people in the picture.

Notes & comments
The same picture can be used to practise the present continuous and is especially good for this kind of transformation:
A man is reading a book. – There's a man reading a book.
It can also be used for making predictions with *going to*, for describing people and for present perfect with *just*.
You may want to make a large copy of the picture to put on the classroom wall and get students to attach examples of the relevant structure.

INSIDE OUT *Resource Pack*

3A *Friday the 13th*

TEACHER'S NOTES

3B Childhood sweethearts

Simone Foster

Type of activity
Reading and speaking. Individual and pair work.

Aims
To practise the past tenses.

Task
To read a jigsaw text and to communicate to find the differences.

Preparation
Make one copy of the worksheet for every two students.

Timing
30–40 minutes.

Procedure
1 Introduce the characters in the text to the class. Explain that they were at school together and that they have been married for 15 years. Tell students that they are going to read an account of how they met.
2 Pre-teach key vocabulary:
   Trisha's story – *a goalkeeper, a goal, a match, a queue, a portion, purse to pay someone back, to chat someone up*
   Ronnie's story – *a goalkeeper, to fancy someone, impatient, grateful*
   Alternatively, students could use dictionaries as they read.
3 Divide the class into two groups – Group A and Group B.
4 Tell the class that they are going to read either Trisha or Ronnie's version of 'How they met'. Explain that they both have a poor memory of how they met and often argue about the details!
5 Put the following questions on the board (see *Answers* on the right).
   1 *Were they friends at school?*
   2 *Did they notice each other at football matches?*
   3 *Where did they first speak?*
   4 *What did Trisha order to eat?*
   5 *Who paid for her food? Why?*
   6 *Who was more interested in their conversation?*
   7 *What happened on the way home?*

   Ask each group to read their 'account' and answer the questions. Explain that the questions are the same for each group.
6 Give out the texts to the relevant groups and give students time to read. Monitor and encourage students in the same group to confer.
7 Re-group students so that an A student sits with a B student.
8 Tell students to go through the questions, exchange answers and find the differences.
9 Students discuss in groups how Trisha and Ronnie's relationship may have developed after that day.

Answers
1 No.
2 **Trisha:** Yes.   **Ronnie:** No
3 In the queue at McDonald's.
4 **Trisha:** Two portions of fries.
   Ronnie: Two burgers and a portion of fries.
5 **Trisha:** Ronnie, because Trisha had no money in her purse.
   Ronnie: Ronnie, because Trisha couldn't find her purse.
6 **Trisha:** Both interested.
   Ronnie: Trisha.
7 **Trisha:** Ronnie kissed her.
   Ronnie: Ronnie gave her a quick kiss.

Follow up
Tell students that Ronnie is now a famous footballer and Trisha is a pop star. Students take the roles of Ronnie and Trisha and a chat show host on a TV chat show. They talk about how they met and what happened in the intervening 15 years.

3B Childhood sweethearts

Trisha's story

I first noticed Ronnie at school when he was in the football team. He was the goalkeeper and I always stood behind the goal when he played but I don't think he knew I was there – he was too interested in the game! I fell in love with him the first time I saw him play.

One day, we all went to Burger King after the match and I was in front of him in the queue. I was very hungry so I ordered two portions of fries. Then, as I was looking in my purse, I realised that I didn't have any money! I felt really embarrassed and asked the assistant to cancel the order. Then I heard a voice behind me saying 'Don't worry, I'll pay for you'. I turned around and looked into his healthy, handsome face. I knew immediately that he was the man I wanted to marry. He said 'You can pay me back next week at the match.'! He chatted me up for a bit and we arranged to see each other at the match the next week. It was raining really hard outside, and he asked me if I wanted to go to his house until the rain stopped. I decided not to go because we didn't really know each other. Then he suddenly kissed me in the rain. It was so romantic!! I ran home and told my mother everything. She smiled and asked if she should buy a hat for the big day!

Ronnie's story

Trisha and I were at the same school in different years. I didn't really notice her but I knew that she liked football because she used to watch our school matches. I was the goalkeeper in the team but she never looked at me. I think she fancied the captain of the team because she was always looking at his legs! Anyway, one week we were all in McDonald's after the match. I was very hungry and I was standing in the queue when I realised that Trisha was in front of me. She ordered two burgers and a portion of fries. Her order took so long that I began to get impatient. I listened to her conversation with the sales assistant. She couldn't find her purse so I offered to pay for her. I didn't expect her to pay me back – girls never do, do they? She was so grateful that she didn't stop talking to me after that. I could see that she liked me but all I wanted was my burger!! When we got outside she followed me home! I had to invite her in because the weather was so wet but she refused. I gave her a quick kiss and said that I would probably see her around. I never thought I'd speak to her again – she just seemed so young and silly!!

TEACHER'S NOTES

4A *Broken sentences*
Priscilla Osborne

Type of activity
Speaking. Group work.

Aims
To review the use of comparatives and vocabulary for describing fitness.

Task
To match parts of broken sentences so that they make one complete sentence.

Preparation
Make one copy of the worksheet for every two students and cut it up as indicated.

Timing
15 minutes.

Procedure
1. Review the comparisons of adjectives presented in unit 4 with the whole class. Remind the students of the *not as ... as* structure.
2. Explain that the task will help the class review the use of comparisons and language for fitness.
3. Divide the class into pairs.
4. Tell the students that each pair will receive sentences divided into two parts. Explain that their task is to make complete sentences from the two halves.
5. Give out one copy of Student A sentence halves to each Student A, and one copy of Student B sentence halves to each Student B.
6. Do the first one as an example with the students. Read out: *People in the UK are living longer ...* and ask the Student Bs to find the correct answer: *... but getting fatter*. Then ask Student Bs to read out the next sentence half: *I'm much fitter ...* and ask the Student As to find the correct half: *... than I was last year*.
7. Circulate and monitor.
8. If necessary, go through the complete sentences with the whole class at the end.

Answers
- People in the UK are living longer but getting fatter.
- I'm much fitter than I was last year.
- Almost 40% of the population never takes any kind of exercise.
- Healthier living and taking exercise makes all of us look and feel better.
- More people join a gym in January than at any other time of the year.
- Doing sport from an early age helps establish good exercise habits for life.
- Walking is one of the best forms of exercise.
- He's not as healthy as he thinks he is.
- It's important to do thirty minutes of exercise three times a week.
- Exercising gently every week is better than exercising very hard but only once a month.
- Playing tennis once or twice a week helps me relax and feel less stressed.
- Many people prefer to watch sport on TV than to take part in any kind of physical activity.
- Swimming is an excellent way of exercising all your muscles.
- Activities such as dancing and skiing make our bones stronger and more dense.
- People should try to do different kinds of physical exercise so that keeping fit doesn't become boring.
- Yoga can be started at any age and at any level of fitness.
- If you're out of condition, don't start with a very intense physical routine.

INSIDE OUT *Resource Pack*

4A *Broken sentences*

| **Student A** || **Student B** ||
End of sentence	Beginning of sentence	End of sentence	Beginning of sentence
	START HERE! People in the UK are living longer …	… exercising all your muscles.	Activities such as dancing and skiing make our bones …
… look and feel better.	More people join a gym in January …	best forms of exercise.	He's not …
… as healthy as he thinks he is.	It's important to do thirty minutes of exercise …	… never takes any kind of exercise.	Healthier living and exercise makes all of us …
… exercising very hard but only once a month.	Playing tennis once or twice a week …	… than at any other time of the year.	Doing sport from an early age …
… helps establish good exercise habits for life.	Walking is one of the …	… but getting fatter.	I'm much fitter …
… stronger and more dense.	People should try to do different kinds of physical exercise so that …	… helps me relax and feel less stressed.	Many people prefer to watch sport on TV than …
… at any level of fitness.	If you're out of condition, don't start with …	… three times a week.	Exercising gently every week is better than …
… than I was last year.	Almost 40% of the population …	… keeping fit doesn't become boring.	Yoga can be started at any age and …
… to take part in any kind of physical activity.	Swimming is an excellent way of …	**FINISH HERE!** … a very intense physical routine.	

© Sue Kay, Vaughan Jones and Philip Kerr, 2002. Published by Macmillan Publishers Limited. This sheet may be photocopied and used within the class.

Photocopiable

TEACHER'S NOTES

4B *Numbers, numbers, numbers*
Jon Hird

Type of activity
Quiz.

Aims
To consolidate and practise numbers and superlatives.

Task
In groups of three, to ask and answer general knowledge/trivia questions.

Preparation
Make one copy of the worksheet per group of three students and cut it up as indicated.

Timing
30 minutes.

Procedure
1 Pre-teach key vocabulary: *life expectancy, linguist, grape, diameter, spin, smell*.
2 Put the students into groups of three and give a different set of questions and answers to each student. The students must not show each other their worksheets.
3 Student A should then read out the first question on his / her list. Students B and C look at their pool of answers and try to agree on the correct answer. The clues (e.g.: *kph, litres, centimetres*, etc.) should help them. Student A writes this down in the 'Answers' column. Then Student B reads out the first question on his / her list and Students A and C try to find the correct answer. The students continue taking turns to ask their questions until all the questions have been asked.
4 Circulate and monitor.
5 Check the answers in open class. The group with the most correct answers is the winner.

Answers
Student A
1 192
2 206
3 63.4 years
4 200,000
5 in the 1850s
6 272 centimetres

Student B
1 250
2 32
3 38 litres
4 1948
5 58°C
6 99.8 metres

Student C
1 100,000 times a day
2 12,756 km
3 25%
4 900 years ago
5 1,670 kph
6 5,000

Notes & comments
Some additional information:

Student A
1 In 2000, there were 192 countries in the world.
2 The adult body has 206 bones, but we are born with 300.
4 This was at the World Cup final in Brazil in 1950.
6 The world's tallest person was Robert Wadlow, an American, who died in 1940.

Student B
1 This is the same as 4.2 babies per second, 360,500 per day or 131,500,000 per year. The population was 6,000,000,000 in the year 2000 and will reach 10,000,000,000 by the year 2050. In contrast, there are only 105 deaths per minute.
2 Frenchman Georges Henri Schmidt is the holder of this record.
4 The shop was opened in California.
5 The hottest temperature ever was recorded at Al' Aziziyah in Libya in 1922.
6 This was at the annual World Grape Throwing Championship. The grape was actually caught by someone in their mouth.

Student C
1 That's the same as 3 billion times in an average lifetime.
3 There are a total of 25 million km of roads on Earth. That's to the moon and back 66 times.
4 Sunglasses were first worn by Chinese judges to hide their eyes so that people couldn't tell what they were thinking.
6 The human nose can only identify about 5,000 of the 17,000 known distinct smells.

INSIDE OUT *Resource Pack*

4B *Numbers, numbers, numbers*

Student A's questions — Answers

1 How many countries are there in the world? _____
2 How many bones are there in the human body? _____
3 What is the world's average life expectancy? _____
4 What was the biggest crowd ever at a football match? _____
5 When did Levi Strauss make the first pair of jeans? _____
6 How tall was the world's tallest human being? _____

Answers to Student B's and C's questions

99.8 metres   32   900 years ago   100,000 times a day   25%   38 litres   58°C
1948   1,670 kph   250   12,756 km   5,000

Student B's questions — Answers

1 How many babies are born per minute in the world? _____
2 How many languages can the best linguist in the world speak? _____
3 How much water is in the adult human body? _____
4 When did the McDonald brothers open their first shop? _____
5 What was the hottest temperature recorded on Earth? _____
6 What's the furthest anyone has thrown a grape? _____

Answers to Student A's and C's questions

200,000   12,756 km   5,000   272 centimetres   206   1,670 kph   63.4 years   192
900 years ago   in the 1850s   25%   100,000 times a day

Student C's questions — Answers

1 How many times does the human heart beat? _____
2 What is the diameter of the Earth? _____
3 What percentage of the world's roads are in the USA? _____
4 When did people first wear sunglasses? _____
5 How fast does the Earth spin? _____
6 How many different smells can the human nose identify? _____

Answers to Student A's and B's questions

1948   250   63.4 years   192   58°C   99.8 metres   in the 1850s   38 litres
272 centimetres   200,000   32   206

© Sue Kay, Vaughan Jones and Philip Kerr, 2002. Published by Macmillan Publishers Limited. This sheet may be photocopied and used within the class.

Photocopiable

TEACHER'S NOTES

5 A few quick questions
Jon Hird

Type of activity
Class mingle and sentence completion.

Aims
To consolidate asking questions and the topics and language from units 1 to 4 of *Inside Out* Pre-intermediate Student's Book.

Task
To complete statements about classmates by mingling and asking questions.

Preparation
Make one copy of the worksheet per student.

Timing
30 minutes.

Procedure
1. Fold the worksheet so only the left column is visible. Give one worksheet to each student.
2. Ask the students to write a different classmate's name on each line in the left column. Alternatively, the worksheet is passed around the class and the students write their own names on the lines. (The latter ensures all students' names appear equally as often)
3. The worksheet is unfolded to reveal incomplete statements about the students' classmates. For example,
   Thierry feels _____ today.
   Emily is named after _____
4. The students mingle around the classroom, asking and answering questions and completing the statements. For example,
   Thierry feels *worried about his exam* today.
   Emily is named after *her grandmother*.
5. Encourage the students to ask further questions to find out more information.
6. When all the sentences have been completed, the students, in pairs or small groups, tell each other what they have learned. Ask the students to report to the class anything interesting they have learned.

Notes & comments
It may be useful to give the students time to prepare the questions they need to ask before they do stage 4. For example: *How do you feel today?, Who are you named after?, Who / Which famous person do you look like?, Who do you have the most rows with?, What is your dream holiday?, How do you keep fit?*

An alternative procedure is for the students to try to guess the responses before they ask the questions. The person who guessed the most correctly is the winner.

INSIDE OUT *Resource Pack*

5 *A few quick questions*

FOLD

_____   feels _____ today.

_____   is named after _____.

_____   thinks he/she looks like _____.

_____   is sometimes called _____ by his/her friends.

_____   's favourite country is _____.

_____   would really like to visit _____.

_____   would love to go on a date with _____.

_____   's favourite celebrity is _____.

_____   's dream holiday is _____.

_____   's favourite sportsperson is _____.

_____   keeps fit by _____.

_____   is the _____ person in the class!

FOLD

© Sue Kay, Vaughan Jones and Philip Kerr, 2002. Published by Macmillan Publishers Limited. This sheet may be photocopied and used within the class. **Photocopiable**

TEACHER'S NOTES

6A *Let's talk!*
Simone Foster

Type of activity
Speaking. Group work.

Aim
To practise using gerunds and infinitives after particular verbs.

Task
To play a board game where students form questions using gerunds and infinitives. These questions form the basis of group discussion.

Preparation
Make one copy of the worksheet for every group of three to five students. Obtain dice and a set of counters for each group.

Timing
30–45 minutes.

Procedure
1. Write two examples on the board – one which requires the gerund and one which requires the infinitive:
   Do you like _____ (go) to the theatre? (going)
   Have you decided _____ (go) out tonight? (to go)
2. Elicit the correct form for each sentence.
3. Divide the class into groups of three to five.
4. Explain the rules of the game:
   - Students throw the dice and move around the board.
   - If they land on a question, the student must form the question correctly using the gerund or infinitive form. The student then asks this question to another member of the group who must give an appropriate answer.
   - If the student lands on a one word prompt, e.g.: DECIDE, then any other member of the group must form a question for the person who landed on that square. The question must use the key word in an appropriate tense and with the correct verb pattern e.g.: *When did you decide to come to England?*
   - The students proceed until someone has finished. If time and inclination allows, they can start again in new groups.

Answers
2. Do you enjoy <u>speaking</u> English?
3. Do you spend a lot of time <u>reading</u> in English?
4. What kinds of music do you hate <u>listening</u> to?
6. What kind of house do you hope <u>to live</u> in when you're 60?
7. Are there any household jobs you can't stand <u>doing</u>?
8. Do you prefer <u>going</u> to the cinema or <u>watching</u> videos?
10. Are there any sports you hate <u>playing</u>?
11. What kind of job do you hope <u>to have</u> in five years time?
13. Do you mind other people <u>smoking</u> next to you in public places?
14. What countries do you want <u>to visit</u> next year?
16. Have you planned <u>to go</u> anywhere on holiday next year?
17. When did you start <u>learning</u> English?
19. What do you love <u>doing</u> on Friday evenings?
20. What sports do you enjoy <u>watching</u> but not <u>playing</u>?
21. Do you mind <u>going</u> to the dentist?
22. Do you generally feel like <u>going out</u> on a wintery day?
23. When was the last time you arranged <u>to meet</u> someone?
25. What do men waste time <u>doing</u> in your country?
27. Is there any food that you don't bother <u>washing</u> before you eat it?

6A Let's talk!

1 START

2 Do you enjoy _____ (speak) English? Give reasons for your answer.

3 Do you spend a lot of time _____ (read) in English? Why/Why not?

4 What kinds of music do you hate _____ (listen) to?

8 Do you prefer _____ (go) to the cinema or _____ (watch) videos?

7 Are there any household jobs you can't stand _____ (do)?

6 What kind of house do you hope _____ (live) in when you're 60?

5 LIKE

9 TRY

10 Are there any sports you hate _____ (play)? Why?

11 What kind of job do you hope _____ (have) in five years time?

12 LEARN

16 Have you planned _____ (go) anywhere on holiday next year?

15 DECIDE

14 What countries do you want _____ (visit) next year?

13 Do you mind other people _____ (smoke) next to you in public places?

17 When did you start _____ (learn) English? Talk about your first teacher.

18 What do you love _____ (do) on Friday evenings?

19 PREFER

20 What sports do you enjoy _____ (watch) but not _____ (play)?

24 HATE

23 When was the last time you arranged _____ (meet) someone? What happened?

22 Do you generally feel like _____ (go out) on a wintery day? Why/Why not?

21 Do you mind _____ (go) to the dentist? Why/Why not?

25 What do men waste time _____ (do) in your country? What about women?

26 ENJOY

27 Is there any food that you don't bother _____ (wash) before you eat it?

28 FINISH

TEACHER'S NOTES

6B *Perfect match*

Simone Foster

Type of activity
Speaking. Class mingle.

Aim
To practise verbs that are followed by the gerund.

Task
To complete information about two friends or relatives and to try to find partners for them.

Preparation
Make one copy of the worksheet for every student.

Timing
25–30 minutes.

Procedure
1 Tell students they are going to complete some information about one female friend or relative and one male friend or relative, who both need new partners.
2 Hand out the worksheets. Do an example on the board. Draw a picture of a (single) friend of yours in a square on the board and write the necessary information to fill the gaps.
3 Ask students to do the same for their two friends or relatives.
4 Demonstrate the activity with a volunteer student. Using the information on the board, talk about your friend and ask the student about his/her possible match:
My friend enjoys cooking and music. What does your friend enjoy doing?
5 Ask students to mingle and exchange information about their friends/relatives. They should try to find suitable partners who have similar interests.
6 At the end of the activity, get some feedback on the 'new couples' and encourage the class to comment on their suitability.

Alternative version
If the students know each other sufficiently well, they could complete the information for another student in the class and then try to 'sell' that student. If they don't know each other well enough, they could interview the student first to find out about their good and bad qualities before trying to 'sell' them.

6B *Perfect match*

All about her

This is _____ .
She is my _____ .

Good qualities
She likes _____ in her free time.
She loves _____ .
She sometimes enjoys _____ with her friends.
She doesn't mind _____ .
She hates _____ .

Bad qualities
She doesn't bother _____ at weekends.
She can't stand _____ .
She spends too much time _____ .
She prefers _____ to _____ .
She wastes time _____ when she is at work.

All about him

This is _____ .
He is my _____ .

Good qualities
He likes _____ in his free time.
He loves _____ .
He sometimes enjoys _____ with his friends.
He doesn't mind _____ .
He hates _____ .

Bad qualities
He doesn't bother _____ at weekends.
He can't stand _____ .
He spends too much time _____ .
He prefers _____ to _____ .
He wastes time _____ when he is at work.

TEACHER'S NOTES

7A Susie's party

Jenny Roden

Type of activity
Speaking. Whole class.

Aims
To reinforce use of the present perfect and past simple. To practise talking about jobs.

Task
To find out, by exchanging information, personal details about a person met at a party. To recall those details.

Preparation
Prepare enough cards for the students in your class. You may want to enlarge them. Some names are specifically male or female, but others can be adapted to suit either sex.

Timing
Up to an hour.

Procedure

1. Ask the students if they have been to a birthday party.
2. Ask what people talk about when they meet for the first time. (Elicit: exchange of personal details, the music, the food, the host/hostess etc.).
3. Explain that they are going to pretend to be at Susie's birthday party. Susie is a model. They all know Susie, but don't all know each other.
4. Give one card to each student. Explain that they have to be the person on the card and that they must ask questions to find out information about the other people at the party.
5. Elicit the questions (see *Answers* below).
6. Elicit what people say when they want to end a conversation, e.g.: *I must get another drink.* or *Oh, there's X, would you excuse me?*
7. The students do the role-play. They are not allowed to write anything down or show each other their cards. Walk around and listen and correct if necessary.
8. Stop the students and let them sit down. Tell them they must try and remember the details they've found out. Tell them it's now one year later. They are going to meet again at Susie's birthday party. They are going to try to tell each other what they remember.
9. Demonstrate with one student:
   I think you're Sam and you're a hairdresser.
   (Remember to add a year to the time they have known Susie).
10. Do the role-play again. (Use name labels if there are a lot of names to remember).

Answers
What's your name?
What do you do? / What's your job?
How long have you known Susie?
Where did you meet her?

Follow up
Ask the students to write down what they know about Susie – her age, her job, her lifestyle, etc. Let them compare notes in pairs/groups and discuss.

7A Susie's party

Name: Sam Peters
Occupation: Hairdresser
How long you have known Susie: 6 months
How you first met: She had an appointment in your salon. She's had her hair done there ever since.

Name: Gabriel/Gabriella Martini
Occupation: Personal assistant
How long you have known Susie: 6 months
How you first met: You came to live next door. Susie invited you in for a cup of tea.

Name: Fatima Omid
Occupation: Housewife
How long you have known Susie: 20 years
How you first met: At school. You were in different classes, but you met at playtime and after school.

Name: Daniel/Daniella Williams
Occupation: Computer programmer
How long you have known Susie: One day.
How you first met: Here at the party. You came with your friend, Tom Morris.

Name: Tom Morris
Occupation: Computer programmer.
How long you have known Susie: 2 years
How you first met: You met her at a disco and asked her out. You have been her boyfriend ever since.

Name: Faizal Omid
Occupation: Truck driver
How long you have known Susie: 6 years
How you first met: Your wife introduced you. She and Susie were best friends at school.

Name: Michel/Michelle Lebrun
Occupation: Photographer
How long you have known Susie: 8 years
How you first met: On a photoshoot. You started chatting and have been good friends ever since.

Name: Frances/Francis Matthews
Occupation: Musician
How long you have known Susie: 5 years
How you first met: You were a friend of Susie's brother.

Name: Jo/Joe Chambers
Occupation: Sales manager
How long you have known Susie: 3 years
How you first met: Susie was promoting one of your products at a show.

Name: Charlie Smith
Occupation: Interior designer
How long you have known Susie: 1 year
How you first met: She used your company to decorate her house.

Name: Chris Glen
Occupation: Teacher
How long you have known Susie: 8 years
How you first met: At college. Susie was on the same course but left to become a model.

Name: Nick/Nicky McAllister
Occupation: Nurse
How long you have known Susie: 4 months
How you first met: Susie broke her finger while she was modelling some sports equipment. You helped to look after her.

Name: Sarah Jacobson
Occupation: Model
How long you have known Susie: 6 months
How you first met: On the same modelling job.

Name: Sandy Beach
Occupation: Chef
How long you have known Susie: 3 years
How you first met: Susie came to eat at your restaurant and loved the food! You've done her catering ever since.

TEACHER'S NOTES

7B Half a conversation

Neil McMahon

Type of activity
Writing and speaking. Pair work.

Aims
To practise present perfect for time up to now and past simple for finished time.

Task
To complete, practise and perform conversations.

Preparation
Make one copy of the worksheet for every four students and cut in half where indicated.

Timing
30 minutes.

Procedure
1. Divide the class into two groups, A and B. Hand out worksheet A to each student in Group A and worksheet B to each student in Group B.
2. Tell students that they are going to read one half of a telephone conversation and they must try to reconstruct the other half. Students could work individually or in pairs within their groups.
3. Tell them to look at Andy's first sentence and imagine what Bob's reply is. They should write Bob's reply in the 'blank conversation' section of the worksheet.
4. Students continue, writing Bob's replies to Andy's remarks. Circulate, checking students are completing Bob's half of the conversation naturally and accurately onto the worksheet. Note down any serious or interesting mistakes for later correction.
5. When students have finished, ask them to tear off the 'blank conversation' section of their worksheet and exchange it with a student from the other group. The students from Group A will now be looking at Group B's 'blank conversation' sections and vice versa.
6. Tell students to read Bob's replies in their new 'blank conversation' sections and imagine what Andy's remarks are. They should then write Andy's remarks on the lines provided in their new 'blank conversation' sections.
7. When all students have finished writing Andy's remarks, ask them to get into pairs with one student from Group A and one student from Group B in each pair. In their pairs, students then check each other's conversations for mistakes and practise reading them aloud.
8. When all pairs have practised the conversations, ask several pairs to perform their for the class.

Follow up
After the students have performed their finished conversations, combine the pairs into groups of four. Ask the students to study the structure of the conversations. Elicit suggestions and write them on the board.
Tell the students they are going to write a complete conversation for homework about a new topic, using the same structure.

Notes & comments
If this is the first time your class has done this type of activity, you may wish to do a complete example first on the board.
Alternatively, you could skip stage 6 so students only create half the conversations themselves.

INSIDE OUT *Resource Pack*

7B *Half a conversation*

Conversation A

Read Andy's conversation and write Bob's replies below.

Andy: Have you seen Angie recently? ..... How is she? ..... Really? What happened? ..... Amazing! ..... No, I haven't. Have you? .....

Conversation B

Read Andy's conversation and write Bob's replies below.

Andy: Have you been on holiday this year? ..... Where did you go? ..... Wow! What did you do there? ..... You lucky man! ..... No, I haven't, but I've heard it's fantastic. What do you think? .....

FOLD

Blank conversation A

Write Bob's replies here. Then tear off this section and swap it with someone from Group B.

Andy: _____
Bob: _____
Andy: _____
Bob: _____
Andy: _____
Bob: _____
Andy: _____
Bob: _____
Andy: _____
Bob: _____

Blank conversation B

Write Bob's replies here. Then tear off this section and swap it with someone from Group A.

Andy: _____
Bob: _____
Andy: _____
Bob: _____
Andy: _____
Bob: _____
Andy: _____
Bob: _____
Andy: _____
Bob: _____

© Sue Kay, Vaughan Jones and Philip Kerr, 2002. Published by Macmillan Publishers Limited. This sheet may be photocopied and used within the class.

Photocopiable

TEACHER'S NOTES

7C Changes

Matthew Jones

Type of activity
Speaking. Pair and group work.

Aims
To practise present perfect for general experience at an unspecified time in the past.

Task
To categorise a range of subjects according to whether they have changed completely, a little, or not at all over the past ten years.

Preparation
Make one photocopy of the worksheet for each student.

Timing
45–60 minutes.

Procedure
1. Write the following three titles, as column headings on the board:
   Has completely changed in the last 10 years
   Has changed a little in the last 10 years
   Hasn't changed at all in the last 10 years
2. Demonstrate the task by discussing one of the subjects in relation to yourself / your opinion and placing the subject in the appropriate column.
3. Either dictate the subjects one by one or tell students to read the subjects and place them in the appropriate column for themselves.
4. Give students time to prepare to justify their category choices.
5. Tell students to interview their partner and complete the second chart for them, giving reasons for their choices.
6. Circulate, monitoring use of present perfect and past simple.
7. Feedback on language.
8. Put students into groups of four to discuss the topics they have put into different columns.
9. If your students are all from the same country, you could then discuss as a class the general topics, e.g. the way people do their jobs, trying to reach consensus on the appropriate columns.

Follow up
Students might predict how these subjects may change in the next ten years.

Notes & comments
To generate maximum participles, intervene where students are not *giving the reasons* for their choices to one another.
Allow *used to* for past states and habits. Highlight form and meaning if necessary.

7C Changes

Subjects

- Pop music
- Fashion in your country
- Your personality
- The cost of living in your country
- The way people do their jobs
- The weather in your country
- Telecommunications
- Family life in your country
- The kind of holidays you like
- Transport in your country
- Your social life
- Television and newspapers in your country
- Education in your country
- Shops in your country
- The things you like to eat and drink
- Sport in your country

YOUR CHART

Has completely changed in the last ten years	Has changed a little in the last ten years	Hasn't changed at all in the last ten years

YOUR PARTNER'S CHART

Has completely changed in the last ten years	Has changed a little in the last ten years	Hasn't changed at all in the last ten years

TEACHER'S NOTES

8A *Thirty-second futures*

Matthew Jones

Type of activity
Speaking. Group work.

Aims
To practise present continuous and *going to* for future arrangements and plans.

Task
To play a board game requiring students to talk about their futures.

Preparation
Make one copy of the worksheet per group of three or four.
Each group will need one coin.
Each student will need one counter.

Timing
30–40 minutes.

Procedure
1. Show students the board game.
2. Demonstrate the task: toss a coin and explain that one side of the coin means *move two spaces*; the other means *move one space*. Move your counter onto a square and speak for 30 seconds on the subject of the square. Encourage questions.
3. Divide the students into groups of three or four. Distribute one board and one coin to each group, and one counter for each student.
4. Students work their way around the board.
5. Circulate, monitoring language and noting down any serious or interesting mistakes for later correction.
6. The activity continues until all or nearly all of the groups have reached the 'Finish'.

Notes & comments
Encourage students to ask further questions of the main speaker on each turn.

INSIDE OUT *Resource Pack*

8A *Thirty-second futures*

START →

FINISH!

Speak for 30 seconds about...

1. Your next holiday
2. Your best friend's ambitions
3. What you're doing this weekend
4. What you are most looking forward to
5. Your next big purchase
6. Your career plans
7. An appointment you must not forget to keep
8. Your next meal
9. Your next journey
10. Your next planned sporting or physical activity
11. Something in the future you are worried about
12. What you are doing after this class
13. The next time you're meeting up with anybody from your family
14. The next clothes you plan to buy
15. Any plans you have to improve your health

© Sue Kay, Vaughan Jones and Philip Kerr, 2002. Published by Macmillan Publishers Limited. This sheet may be photocopied and used within the class.

Photocopiable

TEACHER'S NOTES

8B The root of all evil
Jenny Roden

Type of activity
Short play.

Aims
To practise pronunciation, especially stress and intonation. To reinforce *going to* and the use of the present continuous for the future.

Task
To read and rehearse the play in small groups. To perform the play in groups of four to the other students.

Preparation
Make copies of the worksheet for all the students. Make one 'wad of bank notes' for each group of four students. Cut up paper to represent about ten bank notes. Roll them together to make a wad.

Classroom time
Up to an hour.

Procedure
1 Write the title of the play on the board. Tell the students the saying, *Money is the root of all evil*. Ask them what they think it means (money often brings out the worst in people).
2 Give one copy of the worksheet to each student. Let the students read it. Ask if they think events in the play illustrate the title.
3 Divide the students into groups of four. If the class does not divide equally, students in smaller groups can double up. Alternatively, one student can be the director instead of an actor.
4 Ask the students to take parts and read the play out loud. Explain that the sex of the characters is not important, and *he's* can be changed to *she's* if appropriate.
5 Walk round, helping especially with stress and intonation.
6 If necessary, call the students' attention to the more difficult sentences such as *I know, why don't we share it?* and *To see if anyone's come back to look for it.* and drill.
7 Ask the students to perform the play with actions and props (the 'banknotes'). They may need another rehearsal before the final performance.

Follow up
If the students have enjoyed the activity, let them use a video camera to film it and then watch and comment on their own performance and spoken language.

8B The root of all evil

A What's the matter?

B Look what I've found!

A Money! How much is there?

B Looks like more than 400 quid! Hang on while I count it. (*counts*) £480!

A Where did you find it?

B Just outside in the street. (*moves towards the door*)

A Where are you going?

B To the police station. I'm going to hand it in.

A (*snatches the money*) Wait, you can't do that! You should keep it!

B But it's not mine ... someone may be looking for it right now. (*tries to take the money back*) Here, give it back. I found it! (*they tussle over the money*)

C (*enters*) What's going on? (*A and B stop. A still has the money.*) Where did you get that?

A (*pointing at B*) He/She found it! Just outside!

C What are you going to do with it?

A Keep it. Spend it. ⎫
B Take it to the police station. ⎬ (*together*)

C I know, why don't we share it? Let's go out for a meal.

A Yes, let's buy some new clothes and go to a smart restaurant.

B We can't do that! It isn't ours! Give it back. (*snatches back the money*) I'm taking it to the police station!
(*A and C rush to stop him. D comes in.*)

D What's going on? (*A, B and C stop fighting*) Where did you get that?

A (*pointing at B*) He/She found it! Just outside!

D What are you going to do with it?

B Take it to the police station. ⎫
A Keep it. Spend it! ⎬ (*together*)
C Go out for an expensive meal! Buy new clothes. ⎭

D Hey, you can't keep it. It isn't yours. Let me have it for a minute. (*takes the money and moves towards the door*).

A ⎫
B ⎬ (*together*) Where are you going?
C ⎭

D To see if anyone's come back to look for it.
(*D walks out. A, B and C wait. Half a minute goes by. D doesn't return. They get uneasy*).

A I'm going to see what he's doing. (*goes out. pause. returns, upset*). He's gone! D's gone! He's nowhere to be seen! He's taken the money! He's taken the money!

B ⎫
C ⎬ (*together*) No!

TEACHER'S NOTES

9A Obeying the rules
Jeremy Page

Type of activity
Speaking and writing. Group work and pair work.

Aims
To practise modals of obligation.

Task
To identify and discuss genuine rules.
To produce rules for the class.

Preparation
Make one copy of the worksheet for every two students.

Timing
50 minutes.

Procedure
1 Ask the students if they've ever lived in a different country and, if so, if any of the country's 'rules' were different from what they were used to.
2 Divide the class into pairs. Give one copy of the worksheet to each pair. Explain that the worksheet contains ten rules for living in Britain. Some are true, others are false. Allow a minute or two for the students to read through and check any unknown vocabulary – with you or in dictionaries.
3 Ask the students to try to identify which rules are true and which are false.
4 After ten minutes combine the pairs in groups of four (or six) and ask them to discuss the rules and try to reach an agreement.
5 Ask the groups to report back on their discussion.
6 Once all the groups have reported back, tell them the correct answers.
7 Divide the students into pairs again. Ask them to decide if the answers to the task are exactly the same for their country.
8 Ask the students to report back on any differences between Britain and their country.

Answers
1 True   2 False   3 False   4 False   5 True
6 False 7 True   8 False   9 False   10 False

Follow up
Ask the students to write a set of rules for their class, covering the following topics: punctuality, homework, speaking in their own language, etc.

Notes & comments
This activity works well in both mono- and multi-lingual classes. In mono-lingual classes, be prepared for the students to have different opinions about what is 'normal' for the same country.

9A Obeying the rules

Living in Britain

1 You have to drive on the left.

2 You mustn't use a mobile phone on the bus.

3 You should always wear a hat in public.

4 You should never speak to a stranger on the train.

5 You must never smoke at the cinema.

6 You should always shake hands when you say goodbye to someone.

7 You should usually give a taxi driver a tip.

8 You must always introduce yourself to everyone in a pub.

9 You must never drink tea without milk.

10 You shouldn't eat chocolate in the street.

TEACHER'S NOTES

9B Character crossword

Jon Hird

Type of activity
Crossword.

Aims
To consolidate and practise using character adjectives.

Task
To complete a crossword by identifying opposite character adjectives.

Preparation
One copy of the worksheet per student.

Timing
30 minutes.

Procedure
1 Give one copy of the worksheet to each student.
2 Tell students to complete the crossword using the words on the worksheet and the clues given. Explain that there is only one correct way of completing the crossword, using all the words on the worksheet.

Answers

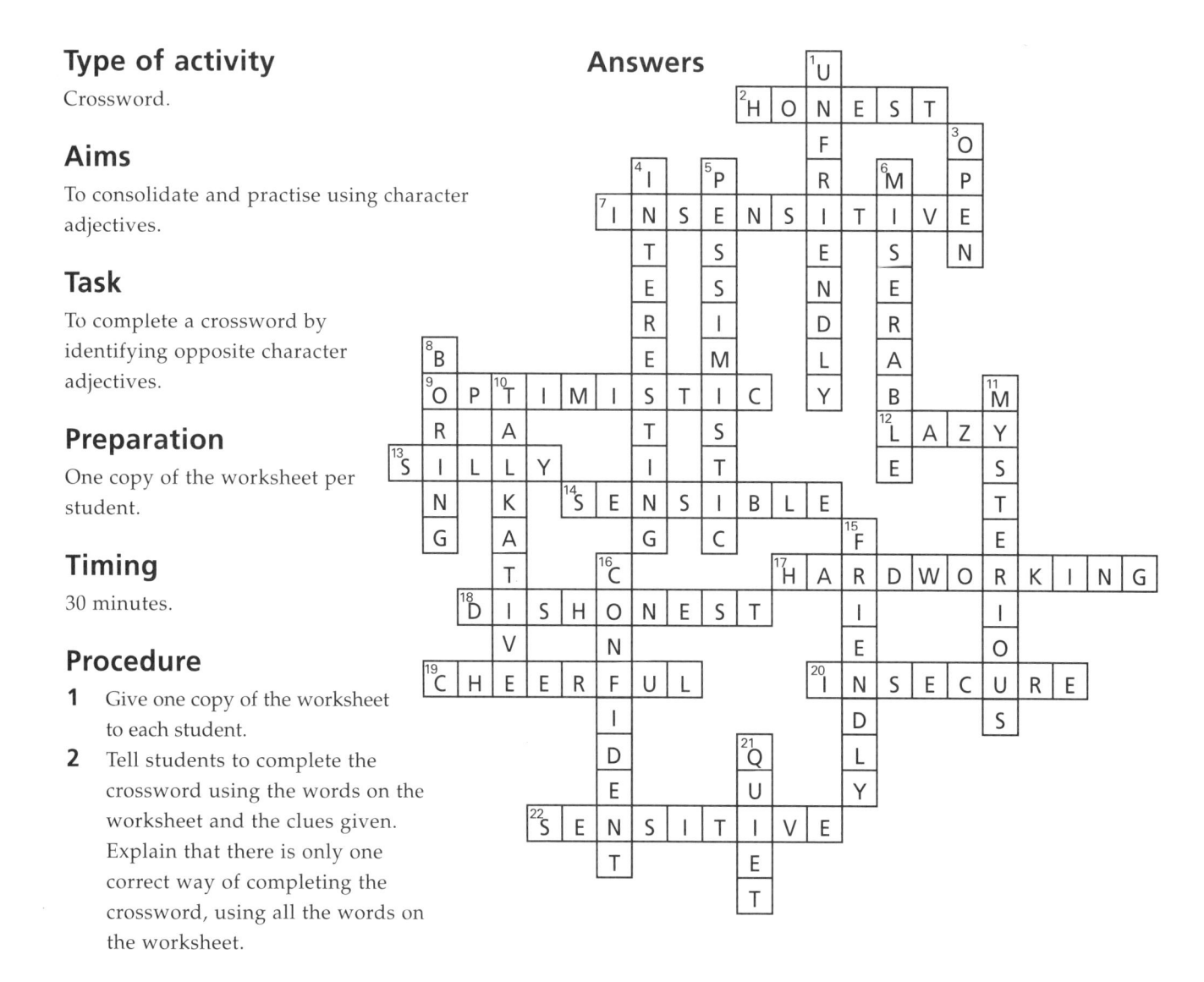

										¹U							
								²H	O	N	E	S	T				
										F				³O			
				⁴I		⁵P				R		⁶M		P			
			⁷I	N	S	E	N	S	I	T	I	V	E				
				T		S				E		S		N			
				E		S				N		E					
				R		I				D		R					
		⁸B		E		M				L		A					
	⁹O	P	¹⁰T	I	M	I	S	T	I	C		Y		B		¹¹M	
		R		A		T		S					¹²L	A	Z	Y	
	¹³S	I	L	L	Y			I					E			S	
		N		K		¹⁴S	E	N	S	I	B	L	E			T	
		G		A				G		C			¹⁵F			E	
				T		¹⁶C				¹⁷H	A	R	D	W	O	R	K	I	N	G
			¹⁸D	I	S	H	O	N	E	S	T		I			I	
				V		N				E						O	
		¹⁹C	H	E	E	R	F	U	L			²⁰I	N	S	E	C	U	R	E
						I				D				S	
				D			²¹Q			L			
				E			U			Y			
			²²S	E	N	S	I	T	I	V	E
				T			E		
							T		

9B *Character crossword*

boring cheerful confident dishonest friendly hardworking honest insecure insensitive interesting lazy miserable mysterious ~~open~~ optimistic pessimistic quiet sensible sensitive silly talkative unfriendly

The following are all opposites:

1 down and 15 down
2 across and 18 across
3 down and 11 down
4 down and 8 down
5 down and 9 across
6 down and 19 across
7 across and 22 across
10 down and 21 down
12 across and 17 across
13 across and 14 across
16 down and 20 across

© Sue Kay, Vaughan Jones and Philip Kerr, 2002. Published by Macmillan Publishers Limited. This sheet may be photocopied and used within the class. Photocopiable

TEACHER'S NOTES

10 What's my job?

Carmen Santos Maldonado

Type of activity
Speaking. Mingling whole class activity.

Aims
To practise adverbs of frequency and job-related questions.

Task
To seek information about one's 'job' and to deduce what it is.

Preparation
Make one copy of the worksheet for every student. Write names of 'jobs' on separate post-it notes. You will need one job and post-it note per student.

Possible examples of jobs:
accountant   bouncer   butcher   clown   dentist
farmer   fashion designer   fireman   gardener
hairdresser   mechanic   musician   nurse
photographer   pilot   plumber   pop star
postman   priest   scientist   soldier   taxi driver
translator   waiter   weather forecaster
window cleaner   writer

Timing
20–25 minutes.

Procedure
1. Pre-teach key vocabulary: *glamorous, prestigious, tips, laboratory*.
2. Explain to the students they are going to be given a job but they will not know what it is. Their task will be to find it out.
3. Give each student a copy of the worksheet. Ask the students to read the instructions and questions.
4. Tell the students to add three extra questions of their own at the bottom. Help with vocabulary problems.
5. Ask the students to come to your desk to get their jobs stuck on their backs.
6. Refer students to the instructions at the top of their sheet. Tell them to mingle freely, asking each person a couple of questions and noting down the answers.
7. Circulate and encourage the use of frequency adverbs in the answers.
8. After 10 minutes of questioning (or when the first student has correctly guessed their job), stop the activity and ask students to write down what they think their job is.
9. Check answers and give feedback.

Follow up
The students can be asked to write about 'their job' for homework: *Positive and negative aspects of being a (taxi driver)*, *My working day as a (taxi driver)*, etc.

Notes & comments
To help students feel more at ease with the activity, you can ask one student to write a job and stick it on your back, and you can circulate as one of the group.

If there is time, you can help students guess their job by giving them clues containing adverbs of frequency, e.g. *You usually meet very important people in your job.*

10 What's my job?

Ask questions to find out about your job and write down the answers. Answer questions about other people's jobs, using the key on the right for your answers. Change partners after every couple of questions.

▶ **Answers**
Yes/no
Yes, all the time
Usually
Very often
Quite often
Sometimes
Not very often
Rarely
Hardly ever
No, never

▶ **Questions**

#	Question	
1	Do I wear special clothes for my job?	
2	Do I often work outdoors?	
3	Do I work with the public?	
4	Do I often work at weekends?	
5	Do I have to travel to do my job?	
6	Do I earn much?	
7	Is my work glamorous or highly prestigious?	
8	Do I work mainly with my hands?	
9	Is my job sometimes dangerous?	
10	Do I often receive tips?	
11	Is my job creative?	
12	Do I work with animals?	
13	Do I work in a laboratory?	
14	Do I usually work in a building? Is it an office?	
15	Do I need to be fit for my job?	
16	Do I need a university degree for my job?	
17	Do I need to be good with numbers?	

Think of three questions of your own and add them to the list:

#		
18		
19		
20		

I think my job is: _____ .

TEACHER'S NOTES

11A Smile!

Peter Maggs

Type of activity
Board game.

Aims
To review lexis from the Student's Book unit by choosing the correct alternative in a sentence.

Task
To play a review game in two teams.

Preparation
Make a copy of the worksheet for each pair of students in the class.
Make a copy of the answers (on the right) for each referee.
Each player/team needs a counter and a dice.

Timing
15 minutes.

Procedure
1. Put your students into groups of three (two players and one referee) or five (two pairs and one referee) and give each group a copy of the worksheet, two counters and a dice. You will need to give the referee a copy of the answers.
2. The students place their counter on the START square and then roll the dice to see who goes first.
3. The students take it in turns to roll the dice, move that number of squares forward and then choose the correct alternative. The referee checks the answers. If correct, the student's counter remains on the square. If incorrect, the student has to return his/her counter to its original square.
4. If a player lands on a SMILE! square, they should move forward but not try to answer the question. If a player lands on an OOPS! square, they automatically miss a go.
5. This continues until a player/pair reaches the final SMILE! square and wins the game.

Answers
See below. The correct answer is underlined.

Follow up
Give a copy of the worksheet to each student in the class and ask them to write out each sentence (with the correct alternative only) for homework.

2 I need to speak/speaking English for my job.
3 She's got long, wavy hair/hairs.
4 He's always telling us what to do – he's very bossy/shy.
6 I can swim/to swim faster than you.
7 He's got freckles/dimples all over his face.
8 He grew a moustache/ beard to cover the scar on his chin.
10 She's got fair hair/eyes.
11 I enjoy watching/to watch sport on TV.
12 He's got pale skin /hair.
14 What does he look like/look?
15 I want being/to be rich.
16 She's wearing false eyelashes/eyebrows!
18 I put on /take off my shoes before I leave the house.
19 She's got the most perfect tooth/teeth.
20 I think I'm going to give up /hang up smoking.
22 He looks tired – he's got bags under his ears/eyes.
23 I'm looking forward to meet/meeting her.
24 She's got a beautiful hair/smile.
26 She feels things very strongly – she's sensitive/sensible.
27 What is she like/look like?
28 When she smiles, small wrists/wrinkles appear next to her eyes.
29 I've decided getting/to get my hair cut.

11A Smile!

1 START	2 I need **to speak/speaking** English for my job.	3 She's got long, wavy **hair/hairs**.	4 He's always telling us what to do – he's very **bossy/shy**.	5 SMILE! Move to Box 7
10 She's got fair **hair/eyes**.	9 OOPS! Miss the next go	8 He grew a **moustache/beard** to cover the scar on his chin.	7 He's got **freckles/dimples** all over his face.	6 I can **swim/to swim** faster than you.
11 I enjoy **watching/to watch** sport on TV.	12 He's got pale **skin/hair**.	13 SMILE! Move to Box 15	14 What does he **look like/look**?	15 I want **being/to be** rich.
20 I think I'm going to **give up/hang up** smoking.	19 She's got the most perfect **tooth/teeth**.	18 I **put on/take off** my shoes before I leave the house.	17 OOPS! Miss the next go	16 She's wearing false **eyelashes/eyebrows**!
21 SMILE! Move to Box 23	22 He looks tired – he's got bags under his **ears/eyes**.	23 I'm looking forward to **meet/meeting** her.	24 She's got a beautiful **hair/smile**.	25 OOPS! Miss the next go
30 SMILE! You're a winner!	29 I've decided **getting/to get** my hair cut.	28 When she smiles small **wrists/wrinkles** appear next to her eyes.	27 What is she **like/look like**?	26 She feels things very strongly – she's **sensitive/sensible**.

> **TEACHER'S NOTES**

11B *Phrasal verb jokes*

Matthew Jones

Type of activity
Reading and speaking. Pair work.

Aims
To revise, practise and expand phrasal verbs.

Task
To match questions and answers of jokes.

Preparation
Make one photocopy of the worksheet for every pair of students and cut it up as indicated.

Timing
40 minutes.

Procedure
1 Tell the students they are going to read some children's jokes. (It may be worth admitting that some children's jokes are *not* hilarious!)
2 Divide the class into Student As and Student Bs and give them the relevant worksheet.
3 Tell students to check they understand the underlined phrasal verbs on their worksheets with other A or B students, with a dictionary, or with yourself.
4 Explain that Student As have the endings for Student Bs' joke openings, and Student Bs have the endings for Student As joke openings. The task is to make complete jokes from the two halves.
5 Do the first one as an example with the students. Read out: *Where do cows go out for the night?* and ask the Student Bs to find the correct ending: *They go out to the moo-vies!*. Then ask Student Bs to read out the next joke: *Which TV channel do bees switch on after work?* and ask the Student As to find the correct ending.
6 Circulate and monitor.
7 When all groups have finished, students read out their complete jokes.

Solution
The jokes are:
Where do cows go out for the night?
– They go out to the moo–vies!
Which TV channel do bees switch on after work?
– The Bee Bee Cee!
What goes up and down but doesn't move?
– The temperature.
Why was Cinderella thrown out of the basketball team?
– Because she ran away from the ball!
Why was the skeleton so lonely?
– Because it had no body to go out with!
Why did the boy throw butter out of the window?
– Because he wanted to see a butterfly!
Why did the belt get sent to jail?
– Because it held up a pair of trousers!
When do bees hum?
– When they run out of words.
Where do bees get on buses?
– At buzz stops!
Doctor, Doctor, I feel like a pair of curtains.
– Well, pull yourself together then!

Follow up
Ask students to rate the three best and three worst jokes.
Ask students to bring in their own jokes and tell them. The other students rank them according to how funny they are.

11B Phrasal verb jokes

Student A

Openings

Where do cows go out for the night?

What goes up and down but doesn't move?

Why was the skeleton so lonely?

Why did the belt get sent to jail?

Where do bees get on buses?

Endings

Because she ran away from the ball.

Well, pull yourself together then!

The Bee Bee Cee.

When they run out of words.

Because he wanted to see a butterfly.

Student B

Openings

Which TV channel do bees switch on after work?

Why was Cinderella thrown out of the basketball team?

Why did the boy throw butter out of the window?

When do bees hum?

Doctor, Doctor, I feel like a pair of curtains.

Endings

The temperature.

Because it held up a pair of trousers.

Because it had no body to go out with.

At buzz stops.

They go out to the moo-vies.

INSIDE OUT Resource Pack

© Sue Kay, Vaughan Jones and Philip Kerr, 2002. Published by Macmillan Publishers Limited. This sheet may be photocopied and used within the class.

Photocopiable

TEACHER'S NOTES

12A *Manifesto*

Simone Foster

Type of activity
Writing and speaking. Group work.

Aims
To practise vocabulary connected with topical issues and to practise the language of expressing opinions.

Task
To write a manifesto for a pressure group and to present it to the class.

Preparation
Make one copy of the worksheet for every group of three to five students

Timing
1 hour.

Procedure
1. Re-elicit the various causes from page 71 of the Student's Book onto the board: *against globalisation; against cruelty to animals; against nuclear weapons; against student fees; against destruction of the environment; against unequal pay for women*
   Encourage them to come up with new ones also.
2. Explain that the students are going to form their own pressure groups connected with the causes from page 71 of the Student's Book or with other causes that they can think of.
3. Divide the students into groups of three to five students.
4. Instruct the students to decide which cause they represent. Tell them to think of a suitable name for their group and to appoint a leader. Explain that the leader will present the group's ideas to the class at the end and that a vote will be taken on the best manifesto.
5. Either draw a skeleton of the manifesto leaflet on the board or photocopy it onto an OHT. Do an example with the class and elicit possibilities to fill the gaps.
6. Give out one worksheet per group and appoint a secretary who will write down the group's ideas.
7. Monitor closely and feed in ideas where necessary.
8. Allow each party leader to present the manifesto to the class.
9. Take a class vote on the best manifesto.

Follow up
The manifestos could form the basis of a poster/leaflet competition. Students could use the basic ideas from the manifestos to produce a more detailed and colourful poster/leaflet for their party. Encourage the use of computer graphics, cut-up magazines, etc.

12A *Manifesto*

MANIFESTO

THE _____ GROUP

Party leader:
_____

FOR
We believe in _____.
We feel very strongly about _____
_____ because
_____.
We support _____
because _____.

AGAINST
We are anti- _____.
We are strongly against _____
because _____.
We are not in favour of _____.

OUR PROPOSALS
We want to ban _____.
We hope to encourage more _____.
We will try to stop people _____.
We will introduce new laws to _____.
We will make _____
and _____ co-operate together more closely.
We promise to _____

Please support us!

> TEACHER'S NOTES

12B Dynamic Replies
Neil McMahon

Type of activity
Speaking. Pair work.

Aims
To practise using verbs in either dynamic or stative forms in common situations.

Task
To reply suitably to given conversation starters.

Preparation
Make one copy of the worksheet for each pair of students and cut in half where indicated.

Timing
20 minutes.

Procedure
1. Write the following sentence on the board: *Did you like that CD I lent you?* Ask students to try to reply, using the verb *think*, for example: *Yes, I think it's brilliant!* Write students' suggestions on the board, responding positively to all possible replies that use *think* correctly.
2. Tell the students they are going to practise responding to similar sentences using specific verbs.
3. Put the students in pairs and give one student in each pair worksheet A and the other student worksheet B.
4. Ask the students to take it in turns to read a sentence aloud. Their partner then has to reply appropriately using one of the verbs shown at the bottom of their worksheet.
5. Circulate, checking students are monitoring each other's responses correctly. Note down mistakes with dynamic and stative verbs for later correction.
6. Conduct feedback in open pairs.

Key
Possible replies for worksheet A:
1. We're thinking of going to …
2. Yes, I saw a film/some friends … etc.
3. I'm having my hair cut/a dinner party … etc.
4. Yes, I can play …/No, I can't play any instruments.
5. Yes! I want …
6. Yeah, everyone likes it./well, I don't like it!
7. I think I look like …
8. Yes. I feel very confident/nervous/anxious … etc.

Possible replies for worksheet B:
1. I see them every weekend/month/twice a year … etc.
2. I feel terrible/awful/sick/fantastic … etc.
3. I started … years ago.
4. He seems really nice/friendly/interesting … etc.
5. Of course! I love it/No! I love animals!
6. I don't know!
7. No. I use it when I want to look up a difficult word.
8. I have an appointment/friend coming round/driving lesson … etc.

Follow up
1. Ask students, in pairs, to choose one of the exchanges and develop it into a longer conversation.
2. Divide the class into groups and ask them to write down as many responses as they can remember. Students then divide the verbs into those they used dynamically and those they used statively.
   Divide the groups into new groups to compare their findings and share different responses.

12B Dynamic Replies

Student A

Read these sentences to student B.

1 Where are you going on holiday?
2 Did you go out last night?
3 What are you doing tomorrow?
4 Are you a musical person?
5 Are you looking forward to Christmas?
6 Football's a very popular sport.
7 You really remind me of someone.
8 Are you ready for the test?

Use these verbs to reply to Student B's sentences.

1 see   2 feel   3 start   4 seem   5 love   6 know   7 look   8 have

Student B

Read these sentences to student A.

1 How often do you visit your relatives?
2 You look awful!
3 How long have you been learning English?
4 What's your new English teacher like?
5 Do you eat meat?
6 What's the capital of Mongolia?
7 Do you often use your dictionary?
8 Will you be at home at 3?

Use these verbs to reply to Student A's sentences.

1 think   2 see   3 have   4 play   5 want   6 like   7 look   8 feel

> TEACHER'S NOTES

13A *Guess my job*

Priscilla Osborne

Type of activity
Speaking. Individual work. Pair work.

Aims
To practise the present perfect continuous and simple.

Task
To talk about the activities and achievements of people in different professions over a period of time.

Preparation
Make one copy of the worksheet for each pair and cut the copies up as indicated.

Timing
15–25 minutes.

Procedure
1 Review the usage of the present perfect continuous and simple with the class.
2 Read out the two examples – the student and the florist. Ask the class to guess what jobs the two people are describing.
3 Divide the class into pairs. Give each Student A a copy of worksheet A and each Student B a copy of worksheet B.
4 Explain that they will take it in turns to describe the daily activities of people in different professions. They must not use the words in the actual job title. So, with the example, the word *flower* cannot be used when describing the *florist's* job. The other student should guess what the job is.
5 Give the students sufficient time to choose the jobs they are most interested in and to prepare a short paragraph describing their daily activities.
6 Circulate and monitor.
7 Note down any serious or interesting mistakes for later correction.

Notes & comments
If the class is confident in their language use, encourage the students to make it difficult for each other to guess what the profession is by describing the more unusual aspects of the job.

13A Guess my job

A

Choose one job from the box below. Describe what you have been doing recently. Can your partner guess what your job is?

Examples

> *University student*
>
> I've been working 18 hours a day recently – my exams are in 2 weeks' time. I haven't been out for weeks now. But I feel quite happy – I've revised almost all the topics – and I haven't got much left to do.

> *Florist*
>
> I've been incredibly busy today – tomorrow is Valentine's Day. I've been making bouquets all day.

a baby sitter   a famous tennis player   a kitchen designer
a nurse   an accountant   a sports journalist
a computer specialist   a shop assistant   a radio newsreader

B

Choose one job from the box below. Describe what you have been doing recently. Can your partner guess what your job is?

Examples

> *University student*
>
> I've been working 18 hours a day recently – my exams are in 2 weeks' time. I haven't been out for weeks now. But I feel quite happy – I've revised almost all the topics – and I haven't got much left to do.

> *Florist*
>
> I've been incredibly busy today – tomorrow is Valentine's Day. I've been making bouquets all day.

a ballet dancer   a waiter   a house-wife/house-husband
a politician   a flight attendant   an artist   a lawyer
a sales representative   a taxi driver

TEACHER'S NOTES

13B *For* and *since*

David Seymour

Type of activity
Speaking/grammar practice.

Aims
To practise questions with *How long ...?* + present perfect simple/continuous, and answers with *for/since*, in the context of lifestyle habits.

Task
Students mingle and complete a worksheet.

Preparation
Make one copy of the worksheet for each student and one for yourself.

Timing
25 minutes.

Procedure

1 Pre-teach vocabulary: *contact lenses, work out (keep fit)*.

2 Hand out one worksheet to each student. Begin by asking a student if he/she lives in a house or a flat. Find out *how long* and fill in the first space on your own worksheet, e.g:
Monica has been living in her flat for six months.
Show the class what you have written.
Now elicit the ending with *since*.
Add below the sentence you have already written:

Monica has been living in her flat since January.
Monica has lived in her flat for six months.

3 Tell the students to stand in the middle of the classroom. Instruct them to complete their worksheets in the same way.

4 When most of the class have finished, ask everyone to sit down again.

5 Elicit questions and answers in the 3rd person singular, e.g.:
T: *Who lives in a flat?*
A: *Monica does.*
B: *How long has she been living there?*
A: *(She's been living there) for six months.*

Encourage the rest of the class to shout out further questions each time, eg:
How much do you pay?
Have you got a view?
Who do you share with? etc.

INSIDE OUT *Resource Pack*

13B *For* and *since*

How long?

Photocopiable

> TEACHER'S NOTES

14A Hello Tom, it's Paula ...

Carmen Santos Maldonado

Type of activity
Speaking. Pair work.

Aims
To practise offers and requests and telephone language.

Task
To make requests and offers over the phone.

Preparation
Make one copy of the worksheet for every pair of students. Cut the copies into columns A and B.

Timing
30–35 minutes.

Procedure

1. Tell your students that they are going to work in pairs, phoning each other up to make requests and offer help.
2. Write on the board or prepare on an OHT:
   Can I speak to Jenny?
   Shall I take the call?
   Could you repeat the number, please?
   Would you mind hanging on a moment?
   Is it okay if I call you back later?
   Would you like me to come straight away?
3. Ask them to copy sentences into their notebooks and then write *offer* or *request* next to each sentence.
4. Elicit ways of starting a phone conversation, and write them on the board, e.g.: *Hello, is John in?*; *It's John speaking.* or *Can I speak to Alison?*
5. Before the pair work, demonstrate the activity with a good student. Role play a short phone call, asking the student to come five minutes early for the next class to help you put some posters up in the classroom.
6. Divide the class into pairs and give each Student A a copy of worksheet A and each Student B a copy of worksheet B.
7. Ask the students to read the instructions on their worksheets. Tell them they should write down the basic requests and offers before starting their conversations.
8. Students follow the instructions on their worksheets to make four telephone conversations.
9. Circulate, checking that students use the appropriate question/answer forms for the offers and requests, and that they are having 'complete' telephone conversations.
10. When most students have finished, ask one or two pairs to act out their conversation for the whole group.

Follow up
The students can be asked to choose two conversations and write them out fully for homework.

Notes & comments
If some pairs finish early, ask them to make offers and requests of their own.

14A Hello Tom, it's Paula ...

A
Use the instructions below to make four phone conversations. You will be asking a favour or making an offer in each conversation.

① Phone with a request
You won't be able to attend your next English class. Phone one of your classmates and ask him/her to collect the homework for you

② Answer the phone
You're learning how to use e-mail and find it a bit difficult. Your cousin is phoning you to offer some help. You accept his offer but would like to use his computer because yours is very slow. You'd prefer to meet during the week.

③ Phone with an offer
One of your colleagues from work is having his car serviced and will be without a car for the next three days. Since you live near him, offer him a lift to work. Arrange a place and time to pick him up.

④ Answer the phone
Your younger sister is phoning you with a request. You're happy to help her, but would like to take your seven-year old daughter with you. You're busy on Saturday morning. Arrange a day and a time to be there.

B
Use the instructions below to make four phone conversations. You will be asking a favour or making an offer in each conversation.

① Answer the phone
One of your English classmates is phoning you with a request. Accept the request and offer to take the homework to your classmate's house. Check his/her address, and arrange a time to go there.

② Phone with an offer
Your cousin is learning about e-mail. You've used e-mail for a while now and want to offer your cousin some help. You are less busy at weekends. Suggest a date and time.

③ Answer the phone
Your car is being serviced during the next three days. You normally drive to work. A colleague is phoning to offer you a lift. Accept the offer, and suggest that you can wait for him/her at the main road. Ask if you can have a lift home too.

④ Phone with an offer
You want to decorate a room in your house this weekend (you'd prefer Saturday morning). Phone your older brother/sister for help. Ask if he/she wants to stay for dinner and check what s/he would like to eat.

TEACHER'S NOTES

14B *Where am I?*

Jenny Roden

Type of activity
Reading and speaking. Pair work.

Aims
To practise informal telephone conversations, requests and giving directions.

Task
To complete the dialogue.

Preparation
Photocopy one copy of the worksheet for each student.

Timing
1 hour.

Procedure
1. Start with a class brainstorm of the language of mobile phoning and text messaging: *signal, breaking up, charging,* etc.
2. Give out the dialogue. Ask the students to read through once to get the gist. Check that students understand the situation. (Tom has got lost on his way to Maria's party.)
3. The students complete the dialogue in pairs. The suggestions for Maria's part can discussed with the whole class. Points to work on are as follows:
   - The directions given by Maria (any directions are suitable here). Check for accuracy.
   - Vocabulary: *lively, amplifier, a search party*
   - Requests: *I wonder if you could do me a favour?*.
4. Once the students have worked on the dialogue in class, they then practise reading it in pairs. While they are doing this, walk around and correct stress and intonation. If necessary, practise as a drill, especially the intonation and stress of exclamations: *Don't say he's lost too! I haven't a clue where I am! Send out a search party!*
5. The students perform the dialogue for each other, either miming the telephone, sitting back to back, or standing apart. The dialogues can be recorded for later analysis.

Answers (suggestions only)
Yes, who's that?
Where are you?
Can you see the name of the pub?
Oh, you're not far away. Turn right.
I said you're not far away. Turn right.
(general directions)
No it's only just started.
Of course, what's that?
But he's not here yet.
All right.
Where are you now?
Can you see the post box?

14B Where am I?

Complete the dialogue.

T = Tom,   M = Maria

T: Hello. Is that Maria?

M: _____

T: It's Tom. I'm lost. I thought was going the right way, but obviously I wasn't.

M: _____

T: At a T-junction, but I haven't a clue where. There's no signpost. I can see a pub on the corner.

M: _____

T: Hang on, let me see ... yes, it's difficult to read in the dark ... yes, it's called *The Queen's Head*.

M: _____

T: I can't hear you! What did you say?

M: _____

T: Turn right. Okay, I'm turning now ... Now what?

M: _____

T: Okay, got that. Am I late for the party? It sounds quite lively there.

M: _____

T: That's good. I wonder if you could do me a favour?

M: _____

T: Tell Mike I've got the amplifier. I sent him a text message, but he didn't reply.

M: _____

T: Not there yet! He said he'd be there early! Don't say he's got lost too! Try his mobile again, will you?

M: _____

T: Fine. If I'm not there in ten minutes, send out a search party!

10 minutes later

T: It's Tom again. You won't believe this! I'm in your street, but I can't find number 82.

M: _____

T: Well, I'm standing outside number 80, but there's no house next to it.

M: _____

T: Yes, yes I can see the post box. Hang on, there's someone coming down the street, I'll ask them. Excuse me, could you ... oh, it's you!

Maria and Tom stand facing each other in the street, both holding their mobile phones and laughing.

TEACHER'S NOTES

15 Find the mistake

Jon Hird

Type of activity
Error correction.

Aims
To consolidate the main language areas covered by units 11 to 14 in *Inside Out* Pre-intermediate Student's Book.

Task
To correct the grammar mistakes in twelve questions and to use these questions for discussion.

Preparation
Make one copy of the worksheet for each pair and cut the copies up as indicated.

Timing
40 minutes.

Procedure
1 Put the students into pairs and give one the Student A worksheet and the other the Student B worksheet. Tell the students that six of the questions contain a grammar mistake and six are correct.
2 Ask the students to work individually to find and correct the grammar mistakes.
3 When they have done this, ask Students A and B to compare the corrections they have made and to identify the correct version of each question.
4 Check answers with the whole class.

Answers
1 What is your favourite song and who <u>was</u> it written by? (Student B)
2 What are you most looking forward to <u>doing</u> in the next few days? (Student A)
3 Do you want <u>to continue</u> to study English after this course? (Student A)
4 What <u>do</u> you <u>think</u> of the number one song at the moment? (Student B)
5 Have you lived in your house <u>for</u> a long time? (Student B)
6 <u>Do</u> you <u>look</u> like anyone famous? (Student A)
7 Where in the world would you most like to go <u>on</u> holiday? (Student A)
8 Do you think <u>you will</u> take an English Language exam in the future? (Student B)
9 How long have you <u>known</u> your best friend? (Student A)
10 How many countries have you <u>been</u> to? (Student B)
11 Can you remember when you <u>had</u> your first kiss? (Student A)
12 How much time do you spend <u>on</u> the internet? (Sentence B)

Follow up
Ask the students, working in pairs or small groups, to ask and answer the questions. Encourage them to ask further questions to find out more information. For example, for question 1: *When did you first hear the song? Why do you like it so much? Does it remind you of a particular time, place or person?*
Ask the students to report back to the class anything interesting from their discussions.

Notes & comments
For Procedure stage 2, you could have the students working in pairs for the initial analysis. This would mean a group of four for Procedure stage 3.

15 Find the mistake

A

Some of these questions contain a grammar mistake. Find the mistakes and correct them.

1. What is it your favourite song and who was it written by?
2. What are you looking forward to doing in the next few days?
3. Do you want to continue studying English after this course?
4. What are you thinking of the number one song at the moment?
5. Have you lived in your house since a long time?
6. Do you look like anyone famous?
7. Where in the world would you most like to go on holiday?
8. Do you think will you take an English Language exam in the future?
9. How long have you known your best friend?
10. How many countries have you ever gone to?
11. Can you remember when you had your first kiss?
12. How much time do you spend at the internet?

B

Some of these questions contain a grammar mistake. Find the mistakes and correct them.

1. What is your favourite song and who was it written by?
2. What are you looking forward to do in the next few days?
3. Do you want continuing studying English after this course?
4. What do you think of the number one song at the moment?
5. Have you lived in your house for a long time?
6. Are you looking like anyone famous?
7. Where in the world would you most like to go at holiday?
8. Do you think you will take an English Language exam in the future?
9. How long have you been knowing your best friend?
10. How many countries have you been to?
11. Can you remember when did you have your first kiss?
12. How much time do you spend on the internet?

TEACHER'S NOTES

16A *Food*

David Seymour

Type of activity
Speaking.

Aims
To improve fluency in speaking.

Task
Students play a board game consisting of topics relating to food.

Preparation
Make one copy of the worksheet for each group of four to five students. Each student will need a counter and each group will need a dice.

Timing
25 minutes.

Procedure
1 Present the unknown vocabulary, e.g.: *starter, utensil, malnutrition*.
2 Hand out the worksheet and dice to each group. Each student needs something small to use as a counter, e.g. a coin. Make sure that someone in the group has a watch.
3 Explain the rules:
 - Students take turns to roll the dice and talk for thirty seconds about whichever topic they land on, without pausing or changing the subject. Tell them that for the purposes of this game, accuracy is not as important as just speaking.
 - If the rest of the group are satisfied that the student has completed the task, he or she wins a point.
 - The first student to get to the Finish gains an extra three points, the next gets two points, and the third gets one. The game ends when the third person finishes.
 - The student with the most points is the winner and gets a prize.

' # 16A Food

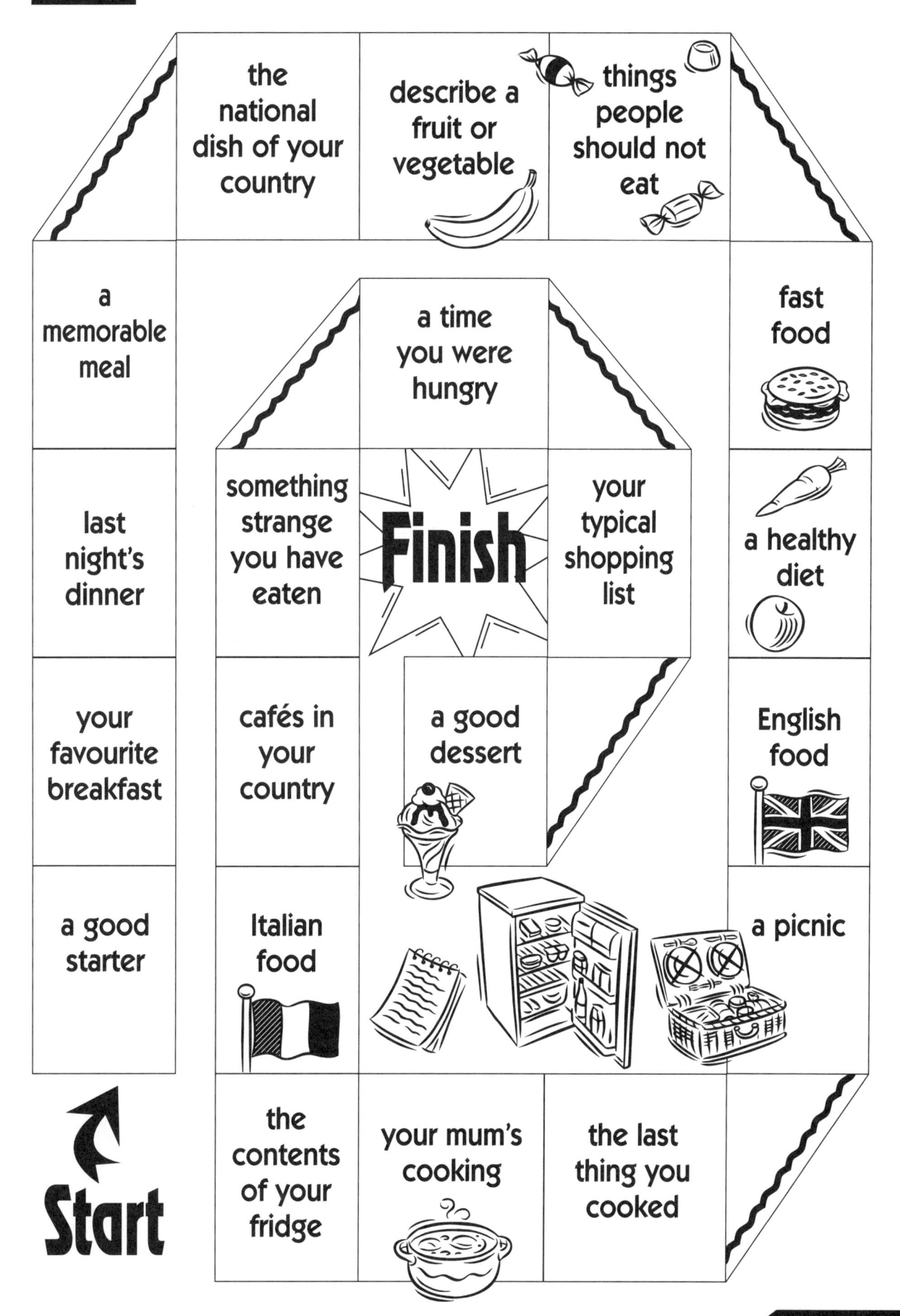

Board game squares:

- the national dish of your country
- describe a fruit or vegetable
- things people should not eat
- a memorable meal
- a time you were hungry
- fast food
- last night's dinner
- something strange you have eaten
- Finish
- your typical shopping list
- a healthy diet
- your favourite breakfast
- cafés in your country
- a good dessert
- English food
- a good starter
- Italian food
- a picnic
- Start
- the contents of your fridge
- your mum's cooking
- the last thing you cooked

TEACHER'S NOTES

16B *Healthy eating*
Priscilla Osborne

Type of activity
Speaking. Group or pair work.

Aims
To practise food vocabulary.

Task
To create a menu for a health farm's restaurant.

Preparation
Make one copy of the worksheet for each pair or group.

Timing
30–45 minutes.

Procedure

1 Review the different ways of cooking (e.g. *grill*; *bake*) and discuss which methods are healthy and which are unhealthy.

2 Ask the students what kind of food they would expect to find on the menu for breakfast at a health farm. Discuss the elements of a healthy diet.

3 Together with the students, brainstorm what might appear on the breakfast menu.

4 Divide the students into pairs or small groups. Hand out one worksheet to each pair or group of students.

5 Ask the students to complete the menu for Celereton Health Farm by creating different healthy dishes for the three remaining meals of the day. They must try to follow the nutritional guidelines given in the worksheet. Tell the students they can use their dictionaries.

6 When they have finished, ask the students to swap menus with each other, compare their results and choose the best one.

16B Healthy eating

Celereton Health Farm

Menu for Sunday 18 August

Breakfast	Organic muesli, organic rolls, home-made jam, fresh fruit salad
	A selection of cheeses and cold meats, boiled eggs Freshly squeezed juice (orange, grapefruit, apple, carrot)
	Tea, coffee, herb teas, fresh milk
Lunch	
Mid-afternoon snack	
Dinner	

Elements of a healthy daily diet

One serving of **protein** (eggs, cheese, soya, meat, fish) – ideally 15% of daily diet.

At least **five** servings of **fruit** and **vegetables** – preferably more vegetables than fruit.

At least **one** serving of **carbohydrate** (potatoes, rice, pulses such as beans and lentils, cereals, bread).

Always try to eat fresh, organic food and avoid processed, ready-prepared, packaged and canned goods.

TEACHER'S NOTES

17A *Homophones*

Peter Maggs

Type of activity
Matching pairs (Pelmanism).

Aims
To identify words with the same sound but different spelling.

Task
To write down two words with the same sound and then play a matching game in two teams.

Preparation
Make a copy of the worksheet for every four students in the class and cut up as indicated.

Timing
20 minutes.

Procedure
1 Read out the following words and ask your students to try to write down two different spellings for each word.
son (*sun*), bare (*bear*), flour (*flower*), week (*weak*), hair (*hare*), sail (*sale*), eight (*ate*), pair (*pear*), mail (*male*), board (*bored*), meat (*meet*), won (*one*).
2 Ask your students to compare what they have written in pairs or small groups.
3 Check in open class. Go through all the words above, checking meaning and pronunciation.
4 Tell your students they are going to play a game in which they have to match two pictures (of the words they have just written) that sound the same (e.g.: *sun* and *son*).
5 Divide the class into pairs and ask one pair to play against another pair. Give each group of four a copy of the worksheet, cut into cards as indicated. Ask them to put all the cards face down on the table.
6 Each team takes it in turns to turn two cards over. The object of the game is to turn over two cards which have the same sound. If a player does this, they keep the pair of cards. As the player turns over the card, they must say the word, otherwise they cannot claim the pair.
7 If the cards are not a matching pair, they are turned over again and left for the next pair to try.
8 The team with the most pairs of cards at the end of the game are the winners.
9 The worksheets can also be used for individual classwork or homework (see *Follow up* stage 1, below).

Follow up
1 Students could follow up the class game by doing the writing and matching activity as homework. Give each student a copy of the worksheet. Ask them to write a word in each box and then match the two words with the same sound by drawing a line connecting them.
2 Ask early finishers to find homophones for these words: way (*weigh*), right (*write*), hear (*here*), red (*read*), wear (*where*), sum (*some*), sew (*so*), there (*their*), for (*four*), by (*bye*).

17A *Homophones*

TEACHER'S NOTES

17B *Animal stories*

David Seymour

Type of activity
Reading and speaking. Grammar recap.

Aims
To develop techniques for improving memory. To find defining relative clauses.

Task
Students read short animal stories, which they then tell each other from memory.

Preparation
Make one copy of the worksheet for each pair of students, plus another copy of the whole worksheet for each student.

Timing
40 minutes.

Procedure
1 Present vocabulary: *wild/tame, to trample, chained, to smash, crew, cargo*
2 Put the students into pairs and give one the elephant story and the other the cow story for silent reading. When they have finished, ask them to put their stories face down and tell their story to their partner from memory.
3 Hand out copies of the complete worksheet. Ask students to underline examples of relative clauses in the stories.
4 Ask the class if they think the stories are true. Does anyone in class know a similar story? If so, ask them to tell it.

Answers
Lovesick elephant
The defining relative clauses are:
… who lived in a small Indian village
… which he gave her
… that is still their home today

Flying cow
The defining relative clauses are:
… which had sunk in the Sea of Japan
… who heard their story
… that was in a field next to a Siberian airfield

Notes & comments
Aesop's fables are good to use in the same way. They also provide an entertaining way of comparing cultures, as the same kind of stories tend to be found in many different places.

17B Animal stories

Lovesick elephant

Madhubala was a tame she-elephant who lived in a small Indian village. One day, she was spotted by a wild bull elephant from the nearby jungle. It was love at first sight. Although Madhubala was chained to a tree, the wild elephant refused to leave her until finally he was chased away by angry villagers. Later that night, the elephant returned, smashed Madhubala's chains and freed her. They ran away into the jungle. Madhubala's keeper, Mahedi Hussain, followed her and a week later brought her back. But Madhubala refused to eat the food which he gave her and trumpeted sadly for her lover. Eventually the wild elephant returned and smashed through walls and houses to reach Madhubala. The reunited couple escaped to the jungle that is still their home today.

Flying cow

Earlier this year, the crew of a Japanese fishing boat which had sunk in the Sea of Japan, were rescued. They claimed that a cow had fallen out of the sky and hit the boat. The officials who heard their story did not believe them, and threw the sailors into prison. They remained in prison for several weeks. Eventually, the Russian Air Force revealed the truth. The crew of one of its cargo planes had stolen a cow that was in a field next to a Siberian airfield. They put the cow in the plane and planned to take it home and sell it. During the flight, the cow panicked and the crew were unable to control it. To save the aircraft and themselves, they pushed the cow out of the plane, just over the Sea of Japan.

TEACHER'S NOTES

18A *Puzzled?*

Matthew Jones

Type of activity
Speaking and grammar. Group work.

Aims
Practice of past perfect and other question forms

Task
To ask *yes/no* questions to solve mysteries.

Preparation
None necessary if the puzzles on the worksheet are dictated.
One copy of worksheet per person if not dictated.

Timing
45 minutes.

Procedure

1 Read out the first puzzle on the worksheet, or give out photocopies.
2 Draw a timeline on the board:

```
―――――――――X――――――――X
  past   man discovered   now
```

3 Tell students they must ask <u>good grammatical</u> *yes/no* questions to discover the explanation behind the strange discovery.
4 Field questions, addressing language problems as they arise. This can best be done by writing the questions asked on the board and analysing them as a class. Establish that questions concerning the time before the discovery of the man will usually need past perfect.
5 Give the following clues when the group begin experiencing difficulties. Do not give all the clues at once: *fire, lake, fire-fighters, helicopters*.
6 When students have solved the first mystery, they can continue with the other puzzles on the page. Again, you can give clues to help students solve the puzzles.

Key

1 The man was a diver. He was diving underwater in a lake near the forest. The forest had caught fire. Helicopters had put the fire out with water from the lake. Accidentally, they had picked up the diver and dropped him in the burning forest with the water.
2 The man had hiccups. When he asked for the glass of water, the barman could hear that he had hiccups. He therefore pulled the gun in order to shock the man and stop the hiccups. It worked, so the man said, 'thank you'.
3 The boxers were women.
4 The wise man told the brothers to swap their horses.

Notes & comments

Allow students time to work in pairs or groups preparing their questions.
You could do this in two teams: give each team two puzzles and the keys to the other two puzzles. They can then ask and answer the other team's questions.

18A Puzzled?

Puzzle 1

In June 1998, a man was discovered in a forest in Australia. The trees in the forest had no leaves. The man was wearing a mask. An ambulance took him to hospital.

> **Ask your teacher *yes/no* questions to discover why the man was there.**
>
> **Example questions:**
> *Was the man wearing a gas mask?*
> *Had he driven to the forest?*

Puzzle 2

A man walked into a bar and asked the barman for a glass of water. The barman pulled out a gun and pointed it at the man. The man said 'Thank you' and walked out.

Puzzle 3

Two boxers were in a boxing match. The fight was scheduled for 12 rounds but ended after 6 rounds, after one boxer knocked out the other boxer. Yet no man threw a punch. How was this possible?

Puzzle 4

A great king told his two sons to race their horses to a distant city. The son with the slower horse would inherit the king's fortune. The brothers didn't know what to do. They asked a wise man for advice. After hearing the advice they jumped on the horses and raced as fast as they could to the city. What did the wise man say?

TEACHER'S NOTES

18B What happened?

Jeremy Page

Type of activity
Writing and speaking. Pair work.

Aims
To practise narrative tenses.

Task
To complete short texts using the correct tense. To sequence a series of events.

Preparation
Make one copy of the worksheet for each pair of students.

Timing
35–40 minutes.

Procedure
1 Ask the students if they have ever had an experience they couldn't explain.
2 Divide the class into pairs and ask them to tell their partner about the experience.
3 Ask if anyone has heard about an especially strange experience. Ask selected students to tell the class what their partner told them.
4 Divide the class into pairs and give one student in each pair worksheet A and the other worksheet B.
5 Ask the students to work individually on the first task: to complete their text using the verbs given in the correct tense: past simple, past continuous or past perfect.
6 When they've finished, ask the students to work individually on the second task: to put the events described in the text in the correct order.
7 Divide the class into two groups: those who've worked on worksheet A and those who've worked on worksheet B. Ask them to compare answers. Monitor both groups and provide correction where necessary.
8 Put the students back into their original pairs and ask them to tell their partner the story they've read.
10 Elicit both stories in open class and check the details.

Answers
Worksheet A
1

1 was travelling	6 gave
2 decided	7 knew
3 had never visited	8 had decided
4 asked	9 had spent
5 checked	10 worked

2
1 e   2 d   3 f   4 a   5 c   6 b

Worksheet B
1

1 was flying	6 landed
2 saw	7 had seen
3 thought	8 had taken
4 was going	9 had broken
5 saw	10 had reached

2
1 b   2 d   3 c   4 a   5 f   6 e

Follow up
Ask the students who have worked on worksheet A to imagine they are George D Bryson and the students who have worked on worksheet B to imagine they are the pilot. Allow them to make notes, then ask them to tell their partner their story in the first person.

18B What happened?

A

1 Complete the text with the correct form of the verb in brackets.

One day, an American businessman called George D Bryson (1) _____ (travel) from St Louis to New York. It was a long journey so he (2) _____ (decide) to stop on the way and spend the night in a town called Louisville. He (3) _____ (never visit) the town before. At the station he (4) _____ (ask) where he could spend the night and was directed to the Brown Hotel. Here, he (5) _____ (check) into room 307 and, for no good reason, asked if there were any messages for him. The receptionist (6) _____ (give) him a letter addressed to Mr George D Bryson, room 307. Of course, this wasn't possible because nobody (7) _____ (know) that Bryson (8) _____ (decide) to spend the night in Louisville at the Brown Hotel. The explanation? The man who (9) _____ (spend) the night before in room 307 was a different George D Bryson! This one was a businessman who (10) _____ (work) in Canada.

2 Put these events into the correct order.

a At Louisville station George D Bryson asked for the name of a good hotel.
b The receptionist gave Bryson a letter addressed to George D Bryson.
c George D Bryson asked if there were any messages for him.
d George D Bryson decided to stay overnight in Louisville.
e George D Bryson, a businessman who worked in Canada, checked into the Brown Hotel.
f George D Bryson, an American businessman, checked into the Brown Hotel.

B

1 Complete the text with the correct form of the verb in brackets.

One day, a pilot (1) _____ (fly) at 1,2000 metres between Delhi and Calcutta when suddenly he (2) _____ (see) an elephant in the sky, flying towards his plane! He (3) _____ (think) he (4) _____ (go) mad, but his co-pilot also (5) _____ (see) the animal. When they (6) _____ (land) in Calcutta, the pilot reported what he (7) _____ (see). The explanation? A religious festival (8) _____ (take) place earlier that day and an enormous balloon of the elephant-god Ganeesh (9) _____ (break) free and (10) _____ (reach) a height of 1,200 metres!

2 Put these events into the correct order.

a The pilot saw an elephant in the sky flying towards his plane.
b A religious festival took place.
c The pilot was flying at 1,200 metres between Delhi and Calcutta.
d An enormous balloon of Ganeesh broke free and reached a height of 1,200 metres.
e The pilot reported what he had seen.
f The co-pilot saw the animal.

TEACHER'S NOTES

19A *Then or now?*

Simone Foster

Type of activity
Speaking. Pair or group work.

Aims
To practise *used to* + infinitive for past habits and states.

Task
To compare past and present lifestyles by discussing contentious statements.

Preparation
Make one copy of the worksheet for each student.

Timing
30 minutes.

Procedure

1 Arouse students' interest by showing them old photographs/a short film clip that depicts life 100 years ago. If you don't have access to such things, then ask students to talk about the lives of their grandparents and how they were different from life now.

2 Write up the first statement on the board with the *I agree / I'm not sure / I disagree* boxes. Invite the students to agree or disagree with the statement and encourage them to give reasons for their choice.

3 Hand out the worksheets and tell the students to do the same with the statements. Allow 5–10 minutes for this stage and make sure the students are working alone. Monitor and help with any difficulties.

4 Divide the class into pairs or groups as you require. Groups will probably lead to more disagreement and ultimately a more productive discussion.

5 Once students have discussed all the statements, conduct a class feedback session focusing on those that proved to be most contentious and any that the students created for themselves that proved interesting.

Follow up

1 The students could write a summary of the opinions expressed in their group.
e.g. *We all felt strongly that ...; The majority of us thought that ...; Some of us said that ..., whereas others said ...; We couldn't agree on ...;* etc.

2 The ideas generated could form the basis of a discursive essay on the advantages and disadvantages of living now as opposed to 70–100 years ago.

3 Photocopy the gapped statements below and hand out one copy for each student/pair. Students complete the statements with their own ideas and then discuss them in groups.

---

1 People are more/less interested in
 _____ .
2 Men are more _____ .
3 People used to have more/less
 _____ .
4 Governments _____
5 Teachers/schools _____
6 There is more/less _____ .

INSIDE OUT *Resource Pack*

19A *Then or now?*

Think about life 100 years ago. Was it better or worse than it is now?

Look at the statements 1–12 below and decide if you agree with them. Tick (✓) the appropriate box to show how you feel. When you have finished, talk to your partner and compare your answers. Try to give reasons for your choices.

One hundred years ago …	agree	not sure	disagree
1 Children used to be happier.			
2 People used to wear better quality clothes.			
3 People used to be fitter.			
4 Family life used to be better.			
5 People used to have more interesting hobbies.			
6 People used to have a better quality of life.			
7 People used to feel safer.			

Nowadays …			
8 People work harder than they used to.			
9 It is more difficult to get around than it used to be.			
10 People have a worse diet than they used to.			
11 Women have worse lives than they used to.			
12 People are less intelligent than they used to be.			

© Sue Kay, Vaughan Jones and Philip Kerr, 2002. Published by Macmillan Publishers Limited. This sheet may be photocopied and used within the class.

Photocopiable

TEACHER'S NOTES

19B *Interview with a centenarian*

Simone Foster

Type of activity
Speaking. Pair work.

Aims
To practise *used to* + infinitive in question and answer forms.

Task
To carry out a role-play in the form of an interview with a centenarian.

Preparation
Make one copy of the worksheet for every two students and cut it up as indicated.

Timing
30–40 minutes.

Procedure

1 Introduce the topic by talking about the students' grandparents/great-grandparents if they have them. If you have access to any old photographs, this could stimulate students' ideas on what life might have been like 70–100 years ago.

2 Pre-teach the words *centenarian, hide and seek* and *learn by rote*.

3 Tell the students that they are going to participate in a role-play with a centenarian. Tell them that a popular magazine wants to write an article about people who are 100 years old or older and that they are sending their reporters to interview them.

4 Divide the class into two groups. Group A will be the reporters and Group B will be the centenarians.

5 Give out the role cards and monitor and help students to prepare their questions/answers. Allow at least 15–20 minutes for this and encourage students to include ideas of their own.

6 Re-group the students into AB pairs and allow students to conduct the role-play.

7 Students could swap roles and improvise the interview again. They shouldn't need any preparation this time around.

Follow up
Students can write the report for the magazine. They will probably need help on how to structure the article. Looking at similar articles written about people's lives would be a good idea. Students could re-do the interview but play the part of their own grandparents.

INSIDE OUT *Resource Pack*

19B *Interview with a centenarian*

Person A

You are a reporter for a magazine. You want to write an article about people who are over 100 years old. Your readers are interested in what life used to be like 70–100 years ago. Use the prompts below to help you make some questions to ask him/her. Use *used to* + infinitive where possible. Add at least one question of your own.

Childhood	**Teenage years**	**Early adulthood**
When and where / born? Where / live as a child? like / school? What games / play? children / happier than they are now? _____ _____	What teenagers / do with their friends? What age / leave school? help around the house? teenagers / have more fun than they do now? _____ _____	What / working conditions / be like? How many children / people / have? What people / do at weekends? How / people / get around? life / easier for families than it is now? _____ _____

✂ ···

Person B

You are over 100 years old!! This is such a special achievement that a magazine wants to write an article about what life used to be like 70–100 years ago. Talk to the reporter about your experiences and what life used to be like. Use the ideas below to help you and use your own ideas.

Childhood	**Teenage years**	**Early adulthood**
Free time: play in the streets / play hide-and-seek / very little pocket money **At home:** no television / play imaginative games / listen to the radio / go to bed early **School:** large classes / no homework / learning by rote / strict teachers / lots of punishments	**Free time:** listen to records / go to dances / go to the cinema / have picnics / go to the seaside on holiday **At home:** lots of servants / fresh food from the garden / helping out around the house / no friends at home **Jobs:** lower school-leaving age / children followed the professions of parents	**At work:** difficult for women to find good jobs / low wages for industrial workers / poor conditions / no holiday or sick pay / better opportunities for rich people **Family life:** large families / support from extended family / family meals / local holidays **Transport:** less traffic / no speed limits / no driving tests / limited public transport

© Sue Kay, Vaughan Jones and Philip Kerr, 2002. Published by Macmillan Publishers Limited. This sheet may be photocopied and used within the class. **Photocopiable**

| TEACHER'S NOTES |

20 Shout it out

Jon Hird

Type of activity
Vocabulary/general knowledge game.

Aims
To consolidate some of the vocabulary and topics from *Inside Out* Pre-intermediate Student's Book

Task
To guess ten given items in various lexical/general knowledge categories, played as a team game.

Preparation
One cut-up and shuffled copy of the worksheet for the teacher and one copy per student to be handed out at the end of the game. A means of timing one minute, for example, an egg timer, a stopwatch, a watch with a second hand.

Timing
30–40 minutes.

Procedure
1 Divide the class into two teams and explain the rules as follows:
   - The teacher selects one of the cards and reads out the category for Team A, for example *School subjects*.
   - The team has one minute to find out the names of the ten items in that category that are on the card. The team members do this by shouting out items, with the teacher telling them *yes* or *no* according to whether or not they are on the card. The items are listed alphabetically to make it easier for the teacher to scan for them. For example,
     Teacher: *School subjects. Go!*
     Students: *Geography?*
     Teacher: *Yes, one point.*
     Students: *Science?*
     Teacher: *No.*
     Students: *Biology?*
     Teacher: *Yes, two points.* etc.
   - The team scores one point for each item they give which is also on the card. They score no points for items which are in the category, but not on the card. If the team gets all ten items, they get 20 points. Record the score for each round.
   - Select a different category for Team B and play again. Then it's Team A's turn again and so on.
   - When all the categories have been used, the team with the most points is the winner.
2 Play the game, with a member of the opposing team timing one minute and shouting *Stop!* when the minute is up.
3 When the game is over, give each student a copy of the worksheet and go through any unfamiliar language and pronunciation that needs dealing with.

Notes & comments
For larger classes, the game can be played with three teams.

For particularly large classes, you could divide the class into several different games with a student in the teacher's role for each game.

The worksheet need not be cut up, and can be used by choosing categories at random and crossing them off as they are used.

The ten words in the *Common words in English* category are actually the ten most common words. The currencies are used in the following countries:
Euro: Ireland, Finland, the Netherlands, Germany, Belgium, Luxembourg, France, Austria, Italy, Spain, Portugal
Dollar: USA, Australia, Canada, Hong Kong, New Zealand, Singapore, Taiwan, Zimbabwe,
Franc: Cameroon, Côte d'Ivoire, Switzerland
Peso: Chile, Colombia, Mexico, Philippines
Pound: UK, Egypt
Riyal: Iran, Saudi Arabia, Qatar
Rouble: Russia
Rupee: India, Pakistan
Yen: Japan
Zloty: Poland

20 Shout it out

Kinds of music	**Shops**	**Items of clothing**	**Big countries**
classical	bookshop	dress	Argentina
country and western	butcher	gloves	Australia
dance	chemist	hat	Brazil
heavy metal	clothes shop	shirt	Canada
jazz	hairdresser	skirt	China
opera	music/CD shop	socks	India
pop	newsagent	tie	Kazakhstan
reggae	sports shop	trousers	Russia
rock	supermarket	T-shirt	Sudan
R'n'B	toy shop	underwear	United States

Jobs	**Currencies**	**Animals in a zoo**	**Makes of car**
actor	Euro	bear	BMW
dentist	Dollar	camel	Cadillac
doctor	Franc	crocodile	Fiat
hairdresser	Peso	elephant	Ford
lawyer	Pound	giraffe	Mercedes
police officer	Riyal	lion	Nissan
shop assistant	Rouble	rhinoceros	Renault
soldier	Rupee	snake	Toyota
teacher	Yen	tiger	Volkswagen
vet	Zloty	zebra	Volvo

The ten commonest words in English	**Languages**	**Sports**	**School subjects**
a	Arabic	athletics	Art
and	English	baseball	Biology
in	French	basketball	Chemistry
is	German	football	Economics
of	Hindi	golf	Foreign language
it	Japanese	motor racing	Geography
that	Latin	swimming	History
the	Portuguese	skiing	Maths
to	Russian	table tennis	Music
was	Spanish	tennis	Physical education

Character adjectives	**Vegetables**	**Parts of the body**	**European football teams**
ambitious	aubergine	arm	Barcelona
boring	bean	chin	Bayern Munich
bossy	carrot	eye	Celtic
confident	cauliflower	head	Inter Milan
friendly	mushroom	knee	Juventus
honest	onion	leg	Liverpool
lazy	pea	nose	Manchester United
optimistic	pepper	shoulder	Paris Saint German
sociable	potato	stomach	PSV Eindhoven
shy	spinach	wrist	Real Madrid